A

Coach's

Nightmare

www.acoachsnightmare.com

Follow on twitter @coachsnightmare

Like us on Facebook

Library of Congress Cataloging-in-Publication Data is available.

ISBN: 978-0-9914414-0-2

Book design by Michael Denison

Author photo by Lynn Marie

II

This book is dedicated to my mother, Debbie. You were always there for me when I needed it the most.

Thanks Ma for everything. I love you

"A man calumniated is doubly injured—first by him who utters the calumny, and then by him who believes it."
Herodotus

A

Coach's Nightmare

By

Frank Grover Jr

PROLOGUE

July 5, 2011, a hot and humid summer night at an old Veterans hall, at seven o'clock; Damien and Sam are the last to arrive. Damien peaks his head out into the hallway to see if anyone else will be attending this meeting.

He slowly turns the cold metal knob with his right hand, and the lock is quietly inserted into the slot. With his left hand on the crease of the door, he slowly pushes it closed; with his right hand on the door knob, he makes sure only a very subtle closing click of the hinge can be heard.

Once Damien closes the door, he turns to Sam and gives him a shrug, letting him know that it's time to start the meeting. By all accounts, Damien knows deep down that this meeting shouldn't happen, but with Sam pulling the strings, he feels that he doesn't have a say in the matter.

Out of a possible twenty two, only eight members of the Board of Directors are in attendance. Most of the Board of

Director meetings that are conducted throughout the year usually have so few members attend. This meeting, just like all the others, seems to be just as irrelevant. Sam and Damien along with Adam, Rodney, and six other members are present.

There is no agenda.

There is no form which is typically passed out prior to the start of any meeting.

It is quite confusing for the members that are here because they have no idea what this meeting could be about.

Sam, as forthright as he usually is, starts to conduct the board meeting.

"As you all can tell, we don't have an agenda for this meeting. To be honest, Damien and I didn't want to leave a paper trail. This meeting is about Frank Grover. What we are about to say cannot leave this meeting, cannot leave this room, and it cannot be discussed with anyone else. We shall not mention it to Frank himself or even talk about it after we conduct this meeting. We did not mention this meeting to Jack, because he and Frank are best friends. If you would like to continue this conversation, go right ahead," Sam looks over towards Damien. Damien nods and begins to speak.

"Lately we have been getting a few phone calls stating that Frank has become an inconvenience. I personally received a phone call from Lisa Jaxon's fiancé, Johnnie, stating how much of a nuisance Frank is to Lisa and her son, Ben. Johnnie called me the other night in an uproar stating that Frank should not be at the ball field where Lisa's son is playing. Even though he was invited to go to the game by a member of the opposing team, Johnnie said that he should know better not to go."

Damien continues, "I was at the game he attended, and, contrary to Johnnie's beliefs, he did not say a word to Lisa or Ben. However, she called her fiancé anyway and started yelling over the phone. Both Frank and I witnessed what she was saying: 'Frank is at the baseball field, and he's causing trouble. He doesn't have a right to be here. I want him out of here immediately. He's right next to the fucking bench. I don't fucking understand why he's at the game and bothering us.'"

"Lisa was making it known to all of us that she was talking about Frank. Frank did nothing wrong. I actually told him to stay because he's free to watch any game he wants. I advised him not to say anything. He never said a word, he knew better not to. He was simply trying to enjoy himself at the game. It's a free country, he should be able to go anywhere without any trouble."

Sam, slightly aggravated with where this conversation is going, abruptly interrupts Damien and states:

"Moving on, there are more important issues at hand that need to be discussed. Frank needs to go to the police and file a report regarding the person who held him up with a knife and robbed him. That person has phone numbers of the parents and coaches of this league. We are afraid he may use those numbers to threaten other parents and coaches or even come down to the field and cause trouble."

Rodney stands up.

"So what if that guy calls? If he does, we can go to the police for harassment. Frank has been in this league for eight years now, and this isn't his fault. With you as a former coach on my team, I am appalled that this meeting is taking place to begin with."

Rodney is furious. His words are starting to jumble up, and he is not thinking about what he is saying.

"What if... What if Frank was kidding about being held up?" He asks.

Everyone starts to talk over each other. Commotion is brought into full gear. A few coaches are saying to one another, what if he was kidding?

Sam speaks once again. "I don't see why Frank would joke about that kind of matter. If he were kidding about being held up, then his state of mind would not be suitable to continue coaching in this league. It would only make the situation more serious. To joke about something like that could mean that he is just trying to get attention, or perhaps losing his mind. If that is the case, we will ask for his resignation immediately."

Rodney, feeling like he put his foot in his mouth, says nothing.

Sam changes the subject. "Johnnie insists that Frank has been talking to Ben against Lisa's permission via text and email."

Now Adam stands up and says, "Do you have proof of this, or is it just hearsay?"

"Well, I don't have proof, only that Johnnie told me these things about Frank." Sam admits.

"As much of a friend that you've been to me, Sam and Damien, this by far is the lowest you guys could possibly go. Lisa also stated that she had a brain tumor and that she should've been

4

dead two years ago. I know this because Frank came to me concerned when they were dating. He didn't know how to react to such a situation, but he talked to me about it. We also witnessed Lisa's outburst during the All-Star game two years ago. Were you even there Sam?" Adam asks.

"No, I wasn't there," Sam responds.

"What about you?" He looks over towards Damien.

"No, I don't recall seeing Lisa's outburst. I don't think I was there." Damien replies.

"We have to look at the facts. In all the years Frank has been here, prior to dating that crazy woman, there have not been any problems at all. Ever since these horrible flyers were put up around the city, this negative perception of Frank has been created. A person assaulted him, and robbed him at knifepoint because of something that's not true. Frank thinks of you guys as his family, and now you are stabbing him right in the back and indirectly saying that he may be a pedophile. This is the lowest any one person can do to their own family." Adam says.

Rodney, absolutely infuriated with the events that are taking place, starts raising his voice in defense of Frank, "We've seen crazy and Lisa fits the profile. So before we make an ungodly assumption, we must gather all the facts, because without them all of this is just a rumor. Are you and Damien stating that he's a pedophile?"

Sam says, "The flyer that was circulating around town stated that he molested children and sold drugs to minors. Based on what I've been told, yes I'm saying that."

Adam stands up extremely irate, "ARE YOU FUCKING KIDDING ME SAM!? You're a lawyer and you're making assumptions? You damn well know that the only clear cut evidence is proof. You are conducting this meeting purely based on assumption. You, of all people should know that's an asinine thing to do. Do you even have any evidence at all?"

"No, we don't have any evidence." Sam admits.

Adam continues, "You are basing this on people's opinions! You don't have any evidence whatsoever. Think about what you are doing. If Lisa is claiming that Frank is conducting this behavior, why hasn't she gone to the police? I'll tell you why, because she's fucking crazy. Frank has been through so much these past couple of years and now we are going to stick a knife in his back and push it as far as we can? What are we going to do about this? He babysat my children for a whole week. If I had any doubt about him as a person I wouldn't have even thought about asking him to babysit my children. Guess what? I never had a problem when he babysat my kids because he wouldn't do anything like that to any child. Yet, here we are talking about him behind his back." Adam is disgusted.

"First of all, he should be at this meeting to not only defend himself but also chime in on what we don't know so he can elaborate on what happened to him. The fact that you decided to conduct this meeting behind his back is just absurd. This league is ruthless, and I am 100 percent by Frank's side because I know he is not capable of such a crime. I witnessed him as a coach day in and day out for many years, and neither one of you, Damien or Sam witnessed that."

"Frank does not deserve this, and you all should be worried that he doesn't turn it around and sue the league for slander, but I will be by his side if he chooses to do so. This league has been nothing but a menace to him. Because of this meeting, I am resigning and so is my wife. I will be removing my kids from the program. I might just tell Frank about this meeting."

"You said you would not talk about this meeting outside of this room." Sam says.

Adam responds, "I never agreed to that. You created this mess, and it has to end somewhere. It's funny how you want Frank to go to the police and report a crime that was committed on him, but you are contradicting yourself, right here, right now, stating that these words shouldn't go out of this room. You and the board members here are witnessing a crime of slander towards Frank and you assume that we shouldn't go to the police!"

"Make up your God damn mind! You're condemning a person for not reporting a crime but you are committing one. Everyone at this meeting should be reporting a crime against you in favor of Frank. Your actions, Sam and Damien make no sense at all." Adam is evidently aggravated.

Rodney rises one last time, "Frank should be at this meeting plain and simple. He's always around my kid and I trust him completely. He's been working at the O'Brien school for the past seven years and hasn't had any problems there. He's the one that was held up with the knife. If anything, this is the time that he needs us the most."

Sam is stubborn as he insists, "Why didn't he go to the police?"

"We don't know why, but if he were here at this meeting we would know, right? We also don't know what he went through, what was said to him. If this person threatened Frank with his life then it's understandable why he would be scared to do so."

Sam is frustrated with the defensive remarks the Board of Directors have in favor of Frank.

"Fine, we will give Frank an ultimatum. Either he goes to the police and files a report on this man or we tell him to resign."

The room quickly goes silent.

The only sound that can be heard is that of the crickets just outside the windows. Everyone is in awe of what just happened. Even Damien doesn't know what to make of the words that just came out of Sam's mouth.

After a long pause, Damien continues for Sam, "Does anyone else have anything to add to this?"

The Board members, still in shock, are unsure of how to react. Everyone looks at one another, slightly shaking their heads no.

"Fine, it's over. We will give Frank an ultimatum later this week and he'll have a decision to make," Sam speaks the final words of the meeting.

The meeting is over. Adam and Rodney with the other six members, even Damien, are in complete shock of what just transpired.

Whispers can be heard as Sam leaves the function hall:

"Since when does Sam have a say in this league? Why is he bossing everyone around?"

"Sam hasn't been involved in the league for quite a few years and now he has become power-hungry."

"Frank does not deserve this at all, especially coming from someone who hasn't seen what he's been going through. This is absolutely insane."

The members agree with one another about the actions that have taken place this evening, but they don't know what to do. They feel like their hands are tied.

CHAPTER ONE

As the sun is finally making its way through the clouds, I'm curious to know where we will be going this afternoon. After downpours soaked the football field, no one knows where we will have to go.

Did the rain change our plans for this afternoon?

Will we have to go to the auditorium?

We all have to check in with the secretary so she can get an official head count of who will be attending the festivities this afternoon. As we start gathering at the function hall, we get word that the ceremony will be taking place outside as originally planned.

As I'm waiting on the thick wet grass with my socks slowly getting soaked, I start making my way towards our designated seats splashing up more water from the field onto my socks. Socks aren't meant to be wet. It just makes me feel uncomfortable. We have to wait here for a couple of hours. On a day of celebration, wet socks will be one of the last things I'll be thinking of.

The anticipation is killing me as I wait to hear my name being called through the speaker on the Crimson Tide High School Football field. As the Superintendent starts to call the names of my classmates, I remember all the bad things that have happened to me while in school; being picked on, tossed around in lockers, being hit with hard covered books, being called Master Splinter and Rat Face; amongst other names, for twelve long agonizing years.

I then recall when it all began.

I remember the first year of being bullied in school. I was in the second grade. I was pushed around and called names. Even at that age, I didn't fight back. My mother always told me violence will never solve anything; it will only make it worse. I thought it would only get better. It never did.

For years thereafter, I was constantly being picked on and bullied. Some years were different than others, but either way I was constantly being bullied for something; whether it was my special needs, my slurring, the way I looked or just being picked last in gym class. There was always something new every day.

I didn't start talking until I was five years old. No one knew why, not even the doctors. To this day, it's one of many things unknown to occur in my life. By the time I entered school, I needed to receive special assistance to help me understand my class subjects. I could never grasp what we were learning in class. Every day I would go to my special needs teacher for an hour, before school was over, so I could try and understand the classes I just attended.

For twelve years I'd dealt with being bullied. Every day I hated going to school. I always thought to myself, what's going to happen to me today? I had buck teeth that would stick out like a rat. Every day there would be someone moving their lips impersonating a rat eating cheese. The bullies would ask me if I had my cheese today.

Some would also ask, "Where are your ninja turtles today, Master Splinter?

One of the punks, Paul, would turn my desk 180 degrees to face the wall. He would do this every day he was in school; he missed school two out of five days of the week. I, on the other hand, had near perfect attendance. Even though I was being picked on every day, I hated missing school because it would take me forever to catch up with whatever school work I had the day before. It was quite evident with my special needs that I needed to attend school every day I could.

Each time Paul would turn my desk, I would immediately turn it back. Once I turned it back, Paul would make sure the teacher wasn't paying attention; he would give me a warning not to do it again by hitting me across the back of my head with his hard covered history text book.

One time when Paul turned my desk, the teacher yelled at me for facing the wall. I told the teacher that Paul was doing it, but he completely ignored my response. He didn't want to do anything about it. He never acknowledged what I told him; he went on teaching his class as if I wasn't even in the room.

The teacher mentioned to us in the beginning of the year that this would be his last year teaching since he was retiring. How he handled this particular situation made it pretty obvious that all he wanted to do was teach. He didn't want to deal with any drama because in less than eight months he would be done with all of it. I never went to anyone else about being bullied. What was the point if no one was listening to me?

For twelve years I endured it. For more than 2,160 days, I've made it this far. The school year lasted 180 days, for the most part. That's the equivalent of being bullied daily for six continuous years, not including when I was made fun of in Cub Scouts or when I played baseball when I was younger. Even though I was constantly being picked on, I never told anyone that I was being made fun of; abused and tossed around like a piñata with everyone getting their turn to give me a whack until I burst.

I never caved in, I never exploded.

I just kept my calm demeanor as I've always done. I knew deep down that the ones who were bullying me would have karma kick them in the ass someday. Most of the bullies were heavily into drugs; cocaine, weed, ecstasy etc. I never tried any drugs. I never drank. I worked hard to the best of my ability in school. One of the bullies while in high school was arrested for selling drugs. I never hated the bullies. I truly believe their parents were to blame. In a way, I felt bad for them, but I knew I couldn't help them. They wouldn't listen to me anyway, so I had to just grin and bear it.

Within minutes it will all be behind me, and I will get to begin another chapter in my life. As I hear my name being called to receive my diploma, I exhale a breath of relief. It's finally over. I get to move on without anybody else picking on me. I grab my diploma and I shake the superintendent of the schools' hand. I head back towards my seat.

After that, the time flies by. Before I know it, the ceremony is over and I head over to see my parents.

On this day of celebration, both my parents are together, which never happens. I walk over to my mother.

"Son, I'm so proud of you."

A few tears start to come from my eyes.

"Are you crying?"

"No, I'm just happy that it's finally over with."

"You've come a long way. You deserve it."

"Yeah, I guess I do."

She has no idea what I've been through. How much I've been bullied. No one knows what I dealt with. She thinks my tears are because I overcame my special needs. That's what she believes, but honestly, it's because I know I won't be bullied ever again. I can finally live my life without worrying about what's going to happen to me. I know every day after today I won't be harassed anymore. Today, June 7, 2000, is the best day of my life.

CHAPTER TWO

Jack Caverly has been my best friend ever since I was seven. He moved to Cambridge shortly after we graduated. I haven't been to his new house since he moved there two years ago.

He was busy with school, and I was busy with work. I didn't really mind going home after work because I started to take care of my mother. I'm a momma's boy. I'm not afraid to admit that. I will always be there for my mother, it's just who I am.

My friend Jack has and will always be my best friend. He's the one person that can always find a way for me to snap out of anything. Right after graduation, I hung out with the wrong crowd. After hanging out with them for a while, I realized that group was trouble especially after I did some stupid things. Once I gave up on those friends, I became a hermit crab. Jack was the one and only person that helped me become social again.

Jack and I have known each other for fifteen years. He's one year older than me. He is 5' 11" and a huge movie buff. He's watched practically anything and everything. He remembers every movie, some word for word. Jack is extremely funny, and without him as my friend, I wouldn't be the person I am today. We have had each other's backs throughout all the dramatic events that we have encountered individually.

I was there for him just last summer. We were in the same bowling league when the news put up a picture of a man that was wanted for stealing Oxycontin at a nearby pharmacy. I get a call from Jack, saying that the police just called him and they wanted him to come in for questioning. I could hear his voice shake, trembling from such accusations. Someone from the bowling alley told the police they thought it was Jack who was stealing the Oxycontin.

I tell him, "I know you didn't do anything wrong, I'm sure it's just a misunderstanding. Just go to the police station and sort out this whole ordeal. I know you wouldn't do a thing like that. Stay calm, you'll be fine, trust me."

"Thanks, Frank. I knew you would understand."

I was the first friend he called. He needed someone to tell him everything was going to be alright. He just needed support, like anyone would in that situation.

Jack calls me back and tells me he called the detective in charge of the case, and he wants him to stop by the station on Friday.

"I'm not going to bowling this week; I have a lot on my mind." He says.

"That's fine Jack, I understand."

As I'm bowling on Thursday night, I notice two police officers coming into the bowling alley. They walk up to a bowler and ask him a question.

That bowler points towards me.

I'm looking around to see if there is anybody else near me. I don't see anyone.

Why would they be looking for me? I didn't do anything, I have no idea what's going on.

The detective starts talking.

"Are you Frank Grover?"

"Yes, I am. Can I help you?"

"We are here to talk about your friend Jack Caverly."

"What about Jack?"

"Someone in this league called us because they believe Jack is the person who's been stealing Oxycontin from the pharmacies."

"There's no way Jack would do anything like that. If you guys did your job right, we wouldn't be having this conversation."

"Don't get smart with us."

"Don't blame my friend for someone else's mistake. I've known him for a long time. I've known him since we were seven. He is a nice kid and he wouldn't lay a finger on anybody let alone steal, yet you have the audacity to blame him."

"We thought we'd ask you so you can tell us what kind of person he is."

"I just told you. You'll find out tomorrow when he stops by to clear his name. Maybe at that point you can apologize too, for not doing your job."

They walk away, aware of the fact that I kept being a smart ass. But to me, it's rightfully so. No one insults my family or friends. If they do, that's when I become a smart ass. It's clearly the best defensive mechanism I have.

Most of the time I'm just being sarcastic, but if I'm a smart ass, it's evident that I don't like what has been said or done.

Jack calls me the following day shortly after coming back from the police station.

"Frank, they told me you were a smart ass to them yesterday."

"Yes I was. I don't care who they are. Even if they were the President of the United States, I would defend my friends especially if I know they are innocent."

"They told me that every time they asked you a question, you always found a way to offend them."

"Obviously if they did their job right, we wouldn't have had that conversation."

"Well, even though you were a smart ass to them, they told me that it's great to see someone defend their friend like that. They said that you're a great friend to have."

"That's just who I am Jack. I've always been there for my friends and nothing will change that. Knowing the kind of person you are, I think I was insulted just as much as you were when someone said it might've been you."

"The detectives said to me, 'Once we saw you walk in, we knew it wasn't you. But we have to tell you what happened when we questioned Frank yesterday.'"

"I think we spent more time talking about you than we did about me being falsely accused. I was able to get one thing to look back on once I was in the station." Jack explains.

"What was that?" I ask.

"I asked them if I could get a mug shot taken just so I can joke about the incident to my friends." Jack replies proudly.

"Did you?"

"Yes I did, you have to see it!"

After that incident occurred, Jack quit bowling in the summer league. He couldn't stand whoever it was that blamed him for something he didn't do. It was easier for him to walk away, he didn't deserve it.

Jack and I will always be there for one another. Since we know each other better than anybody else, we know what one another is capable of doing or not doing. This, to me, is the definition of best friends.

CHAPTER THREE

In the winter of 2003 Jack calls me.

"Frank, I know you love sports just as much I as do. The baseball team that I coach for needs another coach. I was wondering if you would take my place for this year. I can't do it because of my hours at work, and my aunt asked me if I knew of anyone that would like to coach and I thought of you. The season doesn't begin until next year, but I thought I'd ask you now just in case you needed time to think about it. My aunt Melissa and her friend Kim coach the minor Diamondbacks."

As I think about it, I recall the time in 1989 when Jack and I were on the same minor league team. This was how we met one another. His father and his uncle were coaches at the time. Jack's father, Kenny, only cared about having fun; winning was never important, especially at that age. His style of coaching was to make sure each kid played and tried their hardest. We were never a top team, but we were the one team everyone wanted to be a part of.

While on the minor White Sox, I never got a hit. I either walked or struck out. This one time, I hit the ball deep into center field. I ran as fast as I could to first base with my head down. I didn't pay attention to the first base coach, I ran right past him. As I made the turn to go to second base, I looked for the ball, which seemed to be miles away.

The ball dropped into the center fielder's glove. He opened the glove and to my surprise, he caught it. The center fielder jumped ecstatically, amazed he caught the ball. I stood on the base line in complete disbelief. I walked back to the bench with my head down, shaking my head still in shock that the ball was caught. As I grab a seat on the bench, Coach Kenny comes over to me; he puts his hands on my shoulders, lifts my head up and tells me that he's proud of me.

"Frankie, in all the years that you've been here, you never made contact with the ball. For the first three years you always backed out of the batter's box when the pitch would come. But this time, you stayed in the box and you made contact. This just proves that you can hit the ball. I've never seen a ball get hit that far as long as I've been coaching this team. Even though the outfielder caught it, which was amazing to see, I knew you could hit the ball!"

All the parents behind our bench were applauding me. Those parents that had seen me grow with this team the past four years knew about the struggles I had gone through with hitting the ball. If I was lucky, I would foul it off, but I was scared of the pitcher hitting me with the ball so I backed out of the box every time during the pitch. I never made any contact with the ball, except this one time in the minors. I finally hit the ball in fair territory and what Coach Kenny said to me, made an everlasting impression.

Remembering my childhood experience as a baseball player, I wanted to share the same way I was taught by Coach Kenny with anyone I had the opportunity to. Coach Kenny unknowingly inspired me to become a coach and for that reason, I have elected to join the Diamondbacks.

CHAPTER FOUR

I've been an assistant for two years, and even though I enjoy coaching, it's hard to give my input to the head coach, Melissa. I've been helping scout the kids every year as she has asked, but every time she asks for my opinion, she decides to select a kid that she taught in preschool regardless of what I have to say.

My opinion is just something for her to hear, it doesn't have much bearing on who she picks in the draft. Even when it involves putting a player in a certain position on the field, she goes against my opinion when I give it. I don't know why I am coaching a team if I have no input with some of the decisions within the game. I coach because I always have a great attitude towards the game and the players. The players are seven to ten years old. They need direction on how to play. They should be taught how to have fun first, winning will just come naturally after that.

I wish I had more of a say in the matter. I signed up to help coach, not to be ignored. The parents thank me for being such a positive influence. They enjoy my presence as a coach on their child's team. Some have told me I should coach my own team if I have an opportunity. I enjoy coaching and the influence I have on children of instilling good sportsmanship.

For two years during the baseball season, I would go over Melissa's house three times a week, and we would discuss statistics, lineups, and pitching to prepare us for next week.

Since I work well with kids, Kim, who is the boss of the after school-program at the O' Brien school, offers me a part-time job. I could use the extra money. I accept her job offer.

Kim, Melissa, and I plan to see Fever Pitch together. All three of us are avid baseball fans, and since the movie involves the Red Sox, it peaks our interest furthermore. Kim is in her late thirties, and Melissa is in her late fifties. Kim and Melissa have known one another for fifteen years. We set up a Saturday to see the movie with all three of us. At the very last minute Kim cancels, but both Melissa and I agree that we would still see it.

After the movie, her husband is upset with me. He thinks I'm trying to hit on his wife. That was never the case. To be honest, I don't find her attractive. Melissa is thirty years older than me; she's more like a mother to me. But now Melissa's husband thinks I'm trying to hit on her. Something is making him jealous. Whatever it is, I don't want to deal with it.

CHAPTER FIVE

In February of 2007, the major league Giants manager quits right before the seasons' start. With so little time before the season begins, the league scrambles for a new manager to take over.

Personally, I never thought of taking over a team. Even though parents from the minor Diamondbacks suggested that I should be a manager at some point, I never once thought about the majors. From what I heard from the minor league coaches, the major league coaches are very stubborn. It is like going to the dark side, as so many minor league coaches have stated before.

Jack approaches me while we are bowling in the winter league that we've been a part of for eight years, and he says that I should put my name in to be the manager for the Giants.

"No, no I couldn't."

"Yes, you can. They need a manager and if you take over the Giants, I will help you. We will even ask Aaron if he wants to coach as well. I'm sure he will do it."

Aaron and I have been friends for three years. He is an avid sports fan just shy of his twenties. He hates to lose in anything; video games, sport games, poker etc. anything that is competitive. As a former pitcher for his high school baseball team, I felt his presence as a coach would help develop our young players into solid pitchers. He is also in the bowling league.

With the three of us talking about taking over the Giants, Jack says, "Aaron and I understand the decisions that may be discussed during the draft and the coaches meetings that will take place. Plus with my schedule, I'm not sure I can be there every game, but I really want to help. You will be the manager, Aaron and I will be your assistants."

After thinking about it for a couple of minutes, I'm ready to make a decision.

"As part of taking over the Giants, if I get the position, I would like both of you on my coaching staff. As long as both of you agree to be my assistants, I will put my name in for the manager's position."

We all look at each other, nodding our heads with a smile that we all agree. With our mutual agreement, that is when I decide to put my name in to coach the major Giants.

It will also get me away from Melissa's husband thinking I'm hitting on his wife. I don't need someone constantly perceiving something that isn't there. It will be best if I can go up to the majors.

It's 8:30 in the evening.

I'm hesitant to call, I'm not sure if it's too late.

After receiving the final nudge from Jack, I finally call Rob, the president of the league.

"Hello?"

"Hi Rob, this is Frank Grover. I'm calling because I heard the major Giants are looking for a new manager. I've been coaching with Kim and Melissa on the minor Diamondbacks the past three years, and I'm calling to put my name in to be the manager of the Giants."

"Ok Frank, thanks for calling. I will write your name down, and the Board of Directors and I will discuss it. We will let you know in a couple of days."

"Thanks, Rob. I appreciate it."

"No problem Frank."

As I hang up the phone, both Jack and Aaron come up to me.

"So, what did Rob say?"

"We have to wait until the Board of Directors meets to make a decision. He'll call me back in a couple of days to let me know."

Within a couple of days, Rob calls me back.

"Hello?"

"Can I talk to Frank Grover?"

"Speaking sir."

"Frank, the Board of Directors and I have agreed to make you the new manager of the Giants."

"That's awesome! Thank you so much! Is there anything I have to do?"

"Not right now. Considering the season is right around the corner, I took the liberty to call all the parents and tell them what's going on. We can discuss it further when we meet up over the weekend. My son is also on the Giants. It will be easier for me to do everything right now. We will slowly transition you into this process. Is there a good weekend day and time to establish a practice?"

"Any day is fine."

"Let's plan for Saturday at noon and we'll go from there."

"Ok, sounds like a plan. Thanks Rob."

After I hung up with Rob, I then called Jack and Aaron to let them know we will be coaching the Giants.

From what was rumored, Kim and Melissa, who are on the Board of Directors, told me that I was the only coach who signed up to manage the Giants. If it wasn't for Jack and Aaron convincing me to take over the Giants, I'd still be an assistant in the minor leagues.

CHAPTER SIX

We are inheriting a team with eight rookie players and three veterans. The ace of the team is Rob's son.

I knew going into this season that it would be difficult to have all the players adjust to a new coaching staff. With the president of the league having a say on where his kid should play, I knew my first year as the manager of the Giants wouldn't be easy.

Every coach in the majors pinned us to be last in the standings. In the first few weeks, we could barely muster a good game, never mind putting one in the win column. We lost our first six games. It wasn't looking good from the players' point of view, but I knew from the beginning that we would have to make some mid-season adjustments; we didn't know what we had as a team with so little time to prepare for the season. With our ace out with an arm injury; due to his parents forcing him to play in two leagues at the same time, as a team we had to find alternatives.

Since we were out of the race for the Mayor's cup, it was time for the rookies to prove to us what we were looking for.

In this league, all the teams make the playoffs. The best team in the division goes to the Inter-city Mayor's Cup tournament at the end of the season. Once I realized we were out of the Mayor's Cup tournament, I put our focus on giving the rookies a shot to pitch and more importantly, how we could improve for the playoffs. After starting the season 0 – 6, we finally won a game.

Down the stretch, the Giants started to play better as a team, which I expected would happen. Our last ten games, we finished with a 5 – 5 record. Even though the coaches were right that we would finish in last, I felt we were coming on strong at the end of the season.

In the playoffs, it's a double-elimination process. Once a team loses twice, they are out. We knew we had our backs against a wall; we were up against the best ranked team in the playoffs, the Pirates. Everyone knew coming into the playoffs that the Pirates would be the most challenging team to beat. I try to find any motivation I could to win against the Pirates. Once negativity sets in, it creates a snowball effect. I never say anything bad before a game or after it. I sandwich any mistakes with two positives. It's the only way it won't be detrimental to the psyche of the team.

We lose our first game in the playoffs.

We have to win four games in a row to win the championship. That would nearly match our total for the regular season. It's a tough feat to accomplish but not impossible.

We win the next two games. Winning these games gives us confidence heading into the Championship Round.

The Pirates win their first two games; that automatically sends them into the Championship Round. We have to try and beat the Pirates twice to win the Championship.

Our ace is now available to pitch because he has recovered from his arm injury. I am concerned because I'm not sure how this game is going to affect him, but the president of the league, being the father of the ace, demands that I start his son this game with the guarantee that his son will be fine. This will be the last game he will pitch for the major Giants, since he's moving up to Babe Ruth next year.

We are getting every break this game, and the Pirates are falling apart, making error after error. All of our hits land in the right spot every time. Our ace pitches a no-hitter in his final game. It's fitting he ends the season with a no-hitter. Now we must face the Pirates once again, the winner will be crowned playoff champions.

With the Pirates' ace able to pitch the final game of the year, it gives them a slight edge.

The Pirates jump to an early 4 – 0 lead.

The score stays that way until the 5th inning. At the top of the 5th inning, the Pirates' ace shows signs of wearing down, giving up two runs, making it 4 – 2 going into the final inning.

Top of the 6th inning, with this being our last hope, we are giving them everything we've got left in the tank. The score is now 4 - 3 with the bases loaded and two outs.

The number nine batter goes to the plate, through twenty games this whole season he has not had a single hit credited to his stats. Now would be the perfect time to get the first hit of his major league career. With the batter having a full-count, it all comes down to this. I start pacing back and forth, the crowd in high anticipation of what's to come. The pitcher throws the ball; a deep breath is heard from everyone as they await the outcome.

The batter swings with all his might.

Nothing can be heard but silence.

A team erupts in celebration.

All the players surround the star of the game.

The Pirates win the championship. The players crowd the pitcher on the mound.

The batter strikes out swinging for the last out of the game.

Even with the odds against us, with a young team and a rookie coaching staff, we showed resiliency once everyone was comfortable with their role on the team.

I am proud of how this team finished. We were one pitch away from tying the game. Considering how we started the year, we have come a long way. We fell short, but I expect good things to come from this team in the long run.

CHAPTER SEVEN

It's late June 2008, after losing the first game of the playoffs, it's one and done. The league changed the playoff format this year to a one game elimination due to severe weather which prevented us from starting the playoffs on time. We were a solid team, not the best, but we end up finishing with a better record than last year.

At the conclusion of my fifth year coaching in Cambridge, my second year of managing the Giants, Nathan comes up to me.

"Frank, would you like to coach summer baseball this year? It would be for the A team."

Nathan is in his late forties, 6' 4" and a very business-minded individual. He likes to control every situation within the league. Although he is not the president, everyone is aware that he pulls all the strings no matter who is technically in charge. With his twenty-five plus years of service in the league, he's a man who enjoys controlling every situation. He is a very intellectual individual, but even with his Ivy League degree, common sense is still lacking. He can only focus on one item at a time; it is very hard for him to multi-task, when he tries, he gets flustered. It's quite amusing to watch.

I usually accept any opportunity I have to mentor kids in sportsmanship; winning is never the main goal. As long as everyone is having fun, that's all that matters. It will always be my top priority with any team that I coach. That is what Coach Kenny taught me when I was younger. With that in mind, I turn to Nathan.

"Yes, I will coach the A team this year."

I go over to Aaron and Jack to see if they would also like to assist me in the summer, which they agreed to do so.

During the league's usual end-of-the-year meeting, the league tries to determine who will be playing for each division. This year, we have a new president, Damien, and I never see him make a decision. Damien also manages a minor league team. So far as the new president, I haven't seen Damien make an executive decision, I always see Nathan pulling the strings. Nathan reminds me of a Puppet Master, pulling Damien's strings however he chooses.

Every year we are typically the only city-wide division that can construct four summer league teams: The A team, which I have volunteered to coach with Jack and Aaron, consists of the best twelve and eleven-year-olds from the league.

The B team, coached by Jerry and Mr. Loney, consists of the eleven year olds that aren't assigned to the A team as well as the stronger ten-year-old players. Jerry and Mr. Loney coach separate teams in the regular season.

Jerry is in his late fifties and he's been coaching the Nationals for nine years now. Mr. Loney is in his mid-forties and is an assistant to Nathan on the Astros.

The C1 and C2 teams consist of the other ten year olds, and nine year olds that are coming up to the majors next year.

The managers of each team would rank a list of players from 1 – 12. Once the managers rank each player and excluded players from their team, it would be tallied together. If a player didn't make the top twelve, they would be considered an alternate, meaning playing time wasn't guaranteed. Most of the coaches focus on the top twelve players to consistently play. It's unlikely that any coach would ever ask an alternate to play a reasonable amount of time.

Instead of only having players from our division play, Jerry, without my knowledge prior to volunteering to coach the A team, went to the player agent in the Central Cambridge and asked if any of their players would like to participate with our A division.

This originated because Jerry and Mr. Loney devised a plan prior to the conclusion of the regular season to have the best players that were eleven on the B team instead of the A team.

There were six eleven-year-old players that should have been on the A team because of their obvious talent, but Jerry and Mr. Loney wanted them on their B team. Jerry and Mr. Loney convinced themselves that this team, which they wanted, would go all the way and be state champions.

Both Jerry and Mr. Loney were so adamant about their plan that they spoke to Nathan; it's funny how they didn't go to the new President of the League, Damien. After speaking to Nathan, Jerry and Mr. Loney got their wish. In response to this decision, before I could say anything at all, Nathan comes up to me and says: "There are sacrifices that we all have made in this league, we ask you to make a sacrifice this year. Listen, we've been here for twenty plus years, and we've done a lot of sacrificing; it is what it is. Just coach any team we give you."

Nathan isn't coaching in the summer, what gives him the right to tell me what to do? I don't understand why he's making the decisions for everyone else. But nevertheless, without hesitating, I tell Nathan: "I don't care what team I have. I'm still going to coach this team but that's just who I am. It's embarrassing to see how a league will do anything to try and win. It would be easier if you told me ahead of time that we wouldn't have all the players who are deserving of playing for the A team. You might have the coaching experience but clearly you don't care much about sportsmanship."

This was their plan all along. They just needed a coach that would take care of a watered-down team because everyone else didn't want to have a losing season. I made the so-called sacrifice for the league.

As the summer league progresses, I know that my team will have more fun than Jerry and Mr. Loney's B team, even if we are losing. With winning, pressure mounts up and the decisions can become more stressful especially if it's the wrong decision.

Both Jerry and Mr. Loney get aggravated quite easily once they are under pressure. The right coach can lead any team, no matter the talent, into a winning mantra. These two coaches are not the right coaches to lead this team or any team.

It took us, as a league, two weeks to come to an agreement.

Even though Jack, Aaron, and I are coaching this team, we don't have a say in the matter. One thing I am aware of is that it seems no one understands how hard it is for new players, especially from a different part of the city to come into another league where they don't know anybody, to play on a team for only four weeks. It doesn't give the players enough time to get used to one another. That's all I was trying to convey to Nathan, but to no avail.

Central Cambridge has four players that have been nominated to play for our division. Two players are pitchers, and the other two players are infielders.

We still have enough kids to play the summer league without contacting the other division's players. My argument with the league was that we would have to turn away our own players who have played in this league for years. Jerry and Mr. Loney were determined in winning instead of having their own kids from the league play. They would sacrifice the kids being on the streets and getting into trouble, which has always been a concern to the league.

Most of the summer league kids are also being scouted by Babe Ruth coaches during the course of the summer. Any player who gets turned away from playing the summer league would have a harder time reaching Babe Ruth. This is because we, as a league, decided to choose players from another division over our own. I contemplate what to do; I ultimately have the choice to go against the league and not call the four players from the other division.

As fickle as this league is, I will still find a way for everyone to play. It has come to the point that the players from Central Cambridge are excited to play baseball in the summer and I can't turn any of our own players away. I have to find a way to clean up this mess. This is not something I want to get used to doing, especially if it is going to be like this for years to come.

Ultimately, I decide to bring in the other players from Central Cambridge to play with us for the summer league. I couldn't leave anyone who was from our division and has played for six years off the roster, regardless of their talent. At the same time, I couldn't say no to the other kids who had been asked by their player agent to play with us.

I was able to contact three of the four participants via email. Two of them graciously declined to join us due to vacations they have already planned. There was only one contact that did not leave an email address for me to contact them.

I left a voicemail on Lisa Jaxon's phone letting her know that her son Ben had been selected to play with us in the summer.

Lisa called back three hours later. I introduced myself, told her about our schedule and that we would have a practice before the season were to start. It was to be held on June 29th at 6:00 pm.

I then asked Lisa about Ben's pitching and hitting. She told me that Ben was one of the best pitchers in the league. I wasn't sure if it was just a biased opinion, but I could hear the excitement in Lisa's voice that her son was able to play more baseball. I told her: "I am looking forward to coaching your son and I can guarantee you that he will enjoy his summer being on our team."

In the end, only two players decided to play with us from the Central Cambridge. Both Ben and Lenny were highly praised as Central Cambridge's two best pitchers in the league. I opted to have twenty players on the roster, which is the maximum. As always, I do my best to make sure everyone has a chance to play the same amount. Everyone is an all-star.

We have one practice before the summer league begins. The summer league starts one week after our regular season ends. We need this practice to try and get the kids accustomed to one another. More importantly, it will give Jack, Aaron, and I a better perspective of who will be pitching for the A team considering our pitching has been depleted by the B team. We have no idea who will be pitching the first game. With the season being only days away, we need this one practice to determine that.

CHAPTER EIGHT

With dark clouds floating above us, Mother Nature is trying to prevent us from having our only practice before the summer season begins, which is on July 1st. Due to the light rain, I knew that not many players would show up for practice. The weather isn't bad, but many players will not attend practice if the weather doesn't look promising.

Knowing the avid players we have in our division, Jack and I decide to be at the field for a couple of hours just in case players do show up. Rodney and Mr. Baseball also show up to watch the practice. I never called it off because only a misty rain had been falling.

Rodney has been a coach for eleven years. This past year he started to coach in the Majors. He is in his early fifties, has a great sense of humor, and he has a horseshoe of grey hair surrounding his head. Rodney says it how it is; he tends to become aggravated easily, but he warms up after realizing both sides of any situation.

Mr. Baseball has been a coach in the league for twelve years. His keen memory on past games, players, and rules is one-of-a-kind. He is also in his fifties and six feet tall. He is a quiet man, but when it involves the league, any rule change or anything that just does not seem right, he makes his voice heard. Almost everyone in the league will ask him his opinion when it involves the rules and situational plays during games. This is why everyone calls him Mr. Baseball.

As we're all talking about the teams that we have and how last season ended, we see a Black Honda CR-V pull into the right field parking lot. A kid jumps out from the passenger side, opens the trunk to grab his bat bag, and he makes his way towards us. I approach him and introduce myself.

"I'm Frank and you are?"

"I'm Ben, nice to meet you."

"Hi Ben, it's nice to meet you too. Tell me about your season this year."

Ben is ecstatic to tell me that he hit four homeruns and when he pitched, his team went 8 – 0, he struck out at least ten batters in every game. He's very excited to tell me how well he did.

"Ben can you go to the field so the other coaches will start warming you up? I'm just going to talk to your mother so I can introduce myself to her."

"Ok coach, thanks for letting me play on this team."

"You're welcome Ben. Go warm up and when I come down to the field, we'll talk more about your pitching."

I yell out to Jack and Rodney asking if they can start warming up Ben. I tell Ben that Rodney, pointing to the bald man, and Jack with glasses, would start up the practice. I start to make my way towards Ben's mother, who is waiting in the SUV.

As I approach the Honda CR-V, this beautiful red haired, blue-eyed woman is rolling down her window. I introduce myself to her, "I'm Frank Grover. It's nice to meet you."

"I'm Lisa Jaxon. How long will this practice last? I'm surprised you're still holding one."

"It won't last too long. It's only a little water. It all depends who else shows up for practice."

I don't flirt that often, but for some reason, something just clicks during our conversation. We end up talking for a half-hour. Time went by so fast that the other coaches were asking if I was going to participate in this practice I arranged. I was so infatuated with this beautiful woman that I lost track of time.

Anyone in the league, parents or coaches knows I don't typically flirt with anybody. This is a first for me.

Realizing that I need to coach my practice, I politely interrupt Lisa, "I'm sorry but with all due respect, I did arrange this practice, it's only fitting that I conduct it."

"I understand. It was nice talking with you."

"It was nice talking to you as well."

I hand her a schedule of our games.

"As you can see, we have four games a week and our first game is this Tuesday. We are all meeting at this field at 4:00. Can I have your number again, so I can program it in my phone?"

"What happened to my number before?"

"I forgot to program it when I called you, but I want to make sure I have it this time so I know I can call you."

She smiles and adds, "You can call me anytime."

As I walk away, I turn my head towards her. I smile and she does the same. I knew exactly what she was thinking. One day I'll ask her out, but not now, I have to focus on the team.

Only three players show up for the practice; both players from Central Cambridge and one dedicated, avid baseball player from our division. With so few players arriving for the practice, Jack, Aaron, and I need to figure out our best options for pitchers during the summer league.

Considering we had two of the top pitchers from Central Cambridge, we knew that our team's pitching would be solid. The rest was going to be difficult to figure out. In this league, four pitchers is the minimum a team needs to survive. In most cases, the best teams have six or more pitchers to choose from.

CHAPTER NINE

It is July 1st and the A team is getting on the field to practice before the game. The smell of the freshly cut grass looms in the air as everyone runs onto the field. East Cambridge slowly arrives for the first game of the season. Jack, Aaron, and I have agreed to appoint Ben as the starter for the first game of the summer league.

We knew it was going to be either Lenny or Ben for the first game. Both pitchers had more experience this year comparable to the other pitchers we have on the A team.

I call Ben over to tell him the good news.

"You're starting kid, go warm up."

"Really!?" He exclaims.

"Yes, Ben. We picked you to start because we believe you'll do very well. Go out there and just give it your best."

Before I can say anything else, he rushes over to Lisa, jumping with excitement to tell her that he's starting today's game.

I've never seen an audience as big as this before as a coach. The crowds are gathering on both sides of the field. Both stands are filling up; there has to be close to one hundred people here for today's game. This is a game between inter-city rivals. With great anticipation, the crowd, players, and coaches await for the umpires to arrive for the first inter-city matchup of the summer, to start the bragging rights of being the best division in the city.

As the players take the field, nervousness sets in, even for me. I can feel this new sense of urgency. This feeling never gets old for me; our first summer league game, playing new opponents than the normal teams we are used to in our league.

We are pretty excited to see the other teams play. The summer league is known to be very competitive. Now we get to experience first-hand the ups and downs of the summer league. A new chapter begins in learning different styles of baseball from what we are used to.

It doesn't take long for Jack, Aaron, and I to discuss other options for this game at hand. The top of the 1st inning isn't going according to plan, but just like any other game, baseball creates minute by minute decision making. There is never a time that a coach that can create a game plan that will actually pan out precisely; there's always something somewhere that changes it on the fly.

Ben is struggling with his pitches. With no outs and the bases loaded, Ben has created a tough situation for himself, and we have the possibility to pull him from the game. I am patiently waiting to see if he can get out of trouble without my advice.

As the next batter approaches the plate both Jack and I discuss whether or not one of us should go out and talk to Ben. I say to Jack, "Just give him another batter and see what happens."

Ben looks over to see if one of us is going to talk to him. He knows he's struggling. I would've already talked to the pitcher if it were anybody else. Usually I know how people react to adversity, but I didn't know how Ben would react if I went out prematurely. I wanted to see how he would handle this batter. With the bases loaded, no outs, and two runners already crossing the plate, to me, this was the most pressure Ben would have to deal with. I wanted him to show me how he would handle it.

With the sixth batter of the order coming up, Ben is on a tight leash. I have all the confidence in the world in him, but he has to have the confidence within himself to get out of this inning.

Ben's first pitch to the batter hits the batter right in the face. Jack and I, along with the opposing coach, rush over to see if the batter is alright. The batter starts to bleed instantaneously from the nose. Realizing Jack and the opposing coach were controlling this situation, I see Ben throw his glove down in disgust. I quickly run out to the pitcher's mound to talk to Ben during this delay. I have to try and calm Ben down. Just like any kid, once they start struggling, it's hard to come back on their own.

He was starting to get emotional, for two reasons: He felt bad for hitting the batter, and he felt that he was letting his team down.

"Ben, I'm sorry for putting all this pressure on you, I didn't understand how hard it was going to be for you to start a game in front of a team you barely know. I put all the blame on myself."

At first he was shocked that I was blaming myself, his response set the tone for what was to follow.

"What?" he said, slowly.

He didn't seem to know what to say. Ben wasn't prepared for someone else taking the blame. I knew it would be easier on him to blame myself. It takes the pressure off any of the players who feel they've done a disservice to the team.

"Ben, just take your time, relax. I know it's not what you expected, but it doesn't mean you can't change it. You control the game, no one else."

"But I suck."

"You don't suck. It's my fault for putting you in this situation. I take the blame. I put too much pressure on you to do well, but do me one favor."

Ben, with his head down, just wanting this game to be over with, dejectedly asked: "What?"

"I know you can do it, so be the pitcher you were in your division and end this inning! I'm keeping you in the game, it's only 3 – 0 and it's just the first inning. I know you can end this inning, and you'll see that it will get better."

With the ten minute delay that occurred from the batter's injury, I made sure I used every minute of it to settle Ben down. I needed to take his mind off of hitting the batter. The umpire started to make his way from home plate to break up our meeting.

"Ben, let's show your team, parents, and coaches the pitcher you really are. I know you're a great pitcher, there's no doubt about it. I know you can do this. I'm keeping you in the game because I believe you can get us out of this jam."

Ben realizes he's been given a second chance to show everyone how good of a pitcher he really is; his attitude dramatically changes. As I'm slowly walking backwards to our dugout, I can see his confidence building inside him. Right before I turn around, I see him clench a fist and pound it in his glove with excitement and with conviction say, "I can do this."

I believed that I helped Ben calm down and regain his confidence. If I took him out now, it would only be detrimental for him in this game and most likely other games this season. Taking a pitcher out of the game before recording the first out is vastly disappointing to anyone.

As I approached the bench, Lisa says to me, "He's like a little girl, he whines too much."

I simply respond, "I think you would act the same if you just hit someone in the face."

She doesn't say anything else after that comeback.

We are losing early to a 3 – 0 score, and the bases are still loaded with no outs. Ben throws his first pitch since the delay right down the middle, a called strike by the umpire. He turns over to me, and I yell out to him, "just like that kid!"

The count quickly goes 0 – 2 on this batter. Ben winds up his next pitch, the confidence growing more and more after each pitch. With the count 0 – 2 for the first time this game, Ben lets go of the ball from what seems to be too high, but then all of a sudden, the ball drops. The crowd, the opposing team, everyone goes silent. Ben's 12 to 6 curve ball freezes not only the batter but everyone else watching the pitch. The umpire emphatically calls, "STRIKE 3!" Everyone watching is in awe of the perfect curve ball Ben has just thrown.

Players see it from time to time but it is rare. Ben threw three straight strikes, his first strike-out of the game; and with that out, he was transforming into the pitcher everyone knew him to be. There was no hesitation with his next pitches, one right after another. Ben ended the inning by only giving up the three runs and striking out the side. The team surrounded him with confidence after getting out of that jam. He had proved to everyone that he was the pitcher his reputation had him billed as.

Sometimes just a little pep talk gets things going; that's all it seemed he needed.

Ben approaches the bench.

"We're losing coach, I gave up three runs."

"That is true, but with the situation you were in, you only gave up the three runs. You came back and shut them down. We have six opportunities to score runs and it all starts here. Ben, you will start to learn that this team does not give up. That no matter how far behind we get, there will always be resiliency on this team."

After the first inning the score was 3 - 1. Everyone could sense the momentum starting to favor our team. The team's motivation quickly charged into high gear. Top of the 2nd inning, Ben had no trouble this time. He shut down three of the four batters that came up to the plate.

Bottom of the 3rd inning and the score still 3 - 1, a storm was making its way towards us and coming in quickly. As the rain started to fall, we started to rise. Ben's team rallied around him, with a two-run homerun from his teammate Julio, it tied the score at 3 - 3. The rain started to come down even heavier, and with the umpires having the decision to call it, they have not yet done so. Ben was second at bat this inning. He walked then stole second and third. Ben scored the leading run when Andrew hit the double.

We were able to get one more run to make it 5 - 3 with 1 out, and at that point, we saw a vivid flash followed by a loud crash. The storm had centered itself right above us; it started to thunder and lightning continually. We were quickly concerned about the safety of the kids. We rushed over to every player who was not in a vehicle to make sure that we directed them towards one. The opposing coach and I, along with the umpires, convened behind home plate and decided to call it. The game has officially been postponed. We would continue it as part of a double-header next time we play East Cambridge this round.

CHAPTER TEN

As the first round concluded, we finished with a 3 − 3 record, finishing in third place out of four teams. We just missed qualifying for the trophy weekend; the top two teams make it in a four team division. For the most part the team played very well.

Each round has a trophy weekend. There are three rounds, and the top eight teams that have the most points throughout all three rounds go into the Tournament of Champions bracket. After not making it to the trophy weekend in the first round, we have been placed in a different division, most of the teams have close to the same record as we did.

The B team didn't make it to trophy weekend either.

For the second round we have been placed in a six team division. This is rare, but when it does happen, it gives four teams a chance to make it to the trophy weekend. In order to make it to the playoffs we must have at least a 3 − 3 record. Four wins would easily clinch a playoff berth. Our first game is in Framingham. I have asked everyone to arrive at the field by four o'clock.

With most of the games farther away this round, I'm not sure what time we should leave to get to Framingham for a 5:30 game. I don't typically drive in rush hour. Everyone starts to arrive at the field by four o'clock. As we are gathering, I want to avoid the toll road, it's only nine minutes farther than going the Mass Pike route, and I didn't want everyone to have to spend a couple of dollars each for the toll.

Lisa says to me, "Come on, the Mass Pike will be quicker and it's going to be rush hour, the traffic will be worse going your way than if we went the pike. We'll pitch in if you're really worried about the money."

"I really don't care about the money. I just thought that instead of all of us having to pay a toll, we could save ourselves enough money collectively to take the kids out for ice cream after the game."

After being outnumbered; I was pretty much the only one who wanted to go route 9, I finally conceded and decided to go the Mass Pike route. We left at 4:15 with six vehicles altogether. It was just Aaron and I available to coach this game. It started to rain a little bit but nothing to be too concerned about for the game to be postponed; the decision was up to the opposing coach anyway because they are the home team.

As we are driving along the Mass Pike, Aaron and I are discussing our pitching options as well as the batting order for this week. East Cambridge is the only team we have experience playing this round. We want to alter the pitching and batting order. Aaron and I decide that Lenny will be pitching this game against Framingham.

As we arrive at the toll booth, we get a ticket that tells us how much we need to pay according to the exit we take. I don't usually drive on a toll road; I'm not sure how it works. I grab the ticket and hand it to Aaron since I'm driving.

"Aaron, what does it say?"

"I don't know how to read one of these things. What am I looking for?"

"We are taking exit 13, somewhere on that ticket says exit 13 and it matches up with the left side."

"I'm not sure if I'm reading this right, but if I am, you are not going to hear the end of this for a very long time. If the ticket is true on what the price is for the exit, we are going to be laughing at you for years to come. It says that it's only thirty cents." Aaron chuckles.

I'm in disbelief.

"That can't be right, it seems too cheap!"

"I'm used to the tolls being a couple of dollars. The Tobin Bridge is $4.00 per car, how can it only be thirty cents!"

As we approach the toll, I hand the attendant the ticket.

He says, "Thirty cents please."

I look over to Aaron.

"I'm ready for this. I am going to be the laughingstock for the rest of this season."

"That's to say the least. You always find a way for someone to laugh at you." By now, Aaron is hysterical.

We were the first to arrive at the field. Aaron looks over to me and says, "I'm going to stay right here, this is going to be funny."

"I'm ready. I know this is going to be fun."

Everyone is arriving at the same time. I see that Lisa is showing every effort to be the first one to say something to me.

"You were worried about thirty cents! I can't believe you're that cheap." she can barely finish her sentence with her laughter interrupting every word she speaks.

She hands me thirty cents and says, "It was hard for me to find thirty cents, but I had to make sure you had enough money to get back."

She grabs my hand and puts a quarter and a nickel in my palm.

"Now I'm sure you can get home!"

Most of the parents don't say a word; they just laugh as they hand me thirty cents. Lisa on the other hand, can't stop making fun of me. "I'm never going to forget this moment," she says.

"I know, but I really didn't think it was that cheap."

"Well, at least we know how cheap you are."

She can barely breathe with her continuous laughter.

I can't believe I set myself up for that one. But as Aaron said before, I always find a way for people to laugh at me. I'm used to it. For years people have always laughed at me. I've learned to shake it off repeatedly whether or not it's hurtful. This time, it's playfully funny.

I tell Lenny to warm up because he's starting this game. In less than forty-five minutes, three innings fly by with both teams in a scoreless tie. Both pitchers are striking out at least two batters per inning. In the bottom of the 4th inning, Lenny walks the first batter. The runner steals second base, and with a base hit into right field, it brings the runner home to make it 1 – 0 Framingham.

Even though it was not raining, a lightning bolt appeared from the gray sky. The bolt appeared to be very close. There was an intense crash, which made all concerned. Everyone jumped out of their shoes with the sound of the thunder as close as it was.

The umpire instantaneously delayed the game.

With the parking lot a five minute walk, I told the parents to wait for my call as I waited at the field to see if the game would be called off.

Fifteen minutes from when the lightning starts is when the umpire would make the call to officially end the game. The umpire waited patiently, even fifteen minutes past the mark; he officially ended the game.

Framingham won this game 1 – 0 in four innings.

After losing our first game to Framingham, we finished the first week of the second round with a 2 – 2 record.

If we can win the next game then we will go into the trophy round. With a win against East Cambridge and Andover already, we are currently third in the standings, we hold the tie-breaker against East Cambridge due to head to head competition.

If we win against Andover again, we will receive two points for the win and hold the tie-breaker against them. It will make us clinch a playoff spot. At this point, with the extreme weather we are having, it will be hard for the other teams to make up any games. With one game left after Andover, we will be the only team that was able to play all of our scheduled games. We just happened to beat all the rain the past two weeks. If the other games aren't made up prior to the weekend, the standings stay as they are. The trophy weekend must be played according to the schedule. If we beat Andover, we will have three wins. With Andover currently winless, it would all but eliminate them from contention. This is a must win for them.

After making an executive decision, the Commissioner told all the coaches that we need to play the scheduled games for this week, and that the make-up games will not be played. Due to a shortened schedule for the other teams, winning against Andover will seal the deal for us. I'm the only coach on the A team that is aware of this.

CHAPTER ELEVEN

We gather at our field to make it to Andover for a 5:30 game. The players are starting to ask questions on what we need to do to make it to trophy weekend. Knowing that we need to win this game against Andover to clinch a playoff berth, I will do my best not to let anyone know of the situation.

It is a day by day, game by game philosophy that I've always had and will continue to have. I keep telling the players to just worry about today. Some players were able to look on the website to see the standings, but they just weren't sure if it was true that if we won, we would make it.

As I gather everybody before we start our travels, in a circle on the grass, I stand over them and I say, "I know everyone has questions about what we need to do to make it to the trophy weekend. At this time, we are not worried about trophy weekend. We need to focus on today's game. Everyone is playing well. Once this game is over, we will have a better idea of what the future holds for us, but if we keep worrying about what could happen, we won't be focused during today's game, and like I said before, we need to be mentally prepared for every game. Right now, today's game is the only one that matters."

As we arrive in Andover, we notice that there are games being played before us. We have plenty of time to practice, since we arrived early. With all the coaches at this practice; each coach takes the liberty to conduct each facet of the game themselves.

Aaron takes care of the pitching/throwing drills, Jack takes care of the batting practice, and I just oversee the operation and try to figure out the pitching and the lineup for the game.

As I am preparing the lineup for the game, Lisa comes strolling by and wraps her arm around me and says, "I bet you're happy that there wasn't a toll on the way here."

"This will never get old will it?"

"Nope," she says with a smile from ear to ear. "Remember, you did this to yourself."

I close my lineup book and direct my attention towards her. We have plenty of time before the game starts. Every coach is doing well with their practice. It gives me an opportunity to talk to Lisa more.

We barely had a chance to talk after I was deemed the laughingstock of the league. The whole thirty cents fiasco was the perfect icebreaker. We had talked briefly before the games, but I needed to direct my attention to coaching and she understood that. Her interest in me is quite obvious that even the other parents and coaches are asking if we are dating. I always say no, which is the truth, at this point.

58

Lisa says, "Ben is having so much fun with this team and with you as his coach. He's never had this much fun on any team. Central Cambridge was always uptight about winning. You clearly don't care about winning."

"I do care about winning, but I believe one must have fun first. If you're not having fun doing something, you're going to be miserable doing it. Lisa, I may be different from most of the coaches in this league or in any league, but I've always cared about having fun first, that's how I was brought up and that's how I coach."

We talk for thirty minutes, which is all I have time for. The game is about to begin and we need our players to be ready. I'm glad I am able to coach this summer. I'm having more fun than I thought I would. Everyone told me before the summer league started that it was going to be hectic and that it would be too hot and everyone would complain. I have yet to hear a complaint. I'm enjoying this season a lot.

Even though Nathan handed me a watered-down team, I was going to do everything I could to prove them wrong; prove to all the coaches in the league who denied this team that we were having a very enjoyable season regardless of our performance. Once someone tells me I can't do something, that I'm incapable of making it happen, I prove them wrong. That's how I've always been.

Lenny starts the game pitching.

Andover jumps to a four-run first inning lead.

Top of the third inning, we start to make a comeback. With two outs and runners on 1st and 2nd, Lenny comes to the plate, and on the very first pitch, he hits a three-run homerun to make it a one-run game. With that homerun, the players are starting to feel the anticipation of possibly making the playoffs; they know that in order to have a chance, winning this game would be important, but I didn't tell them that we would be in if we won. Lenny pitches a 1-2-3 inning in the bottom of the third.

Top of the 4th inning, the weather has different plans of its own. All of a sudden the rain starts to come down pretty steadily. The first batter up this inning is having trouble seeing the ball, he strikes out on the first three pitches; he swings at all of them because he can't see the ball. As the inning progresses; the rain follows suit. It is now coming down very heavily; puddles are starting to form at the pitchers' mound and home plate. Water is starting to pour into the dugout, but the umpires have yet to delay or postpone the game. If we don't get a run this inning, the umpires could call the game. After four innings, the game is official.

With Andover leading 4 – 3, they would win because they are the home team and we would've played four innings. Andover would then still have a chance to make the trophy weekend. There is nothing I can do at this point, we aren't the home team, and the umpires seem to be home town favorites; the odds are against us.

Ben arrives at the plate. With the rain continuing to blind the batters, it's hard seeing the ball. Deep down I know it's going to be hard to fight such obstacles, but I must convince the team and the players, that anything is possible, anything can happen.

After the first pitch, the umpire calls a strike. Watching the pitch myself, I can barely see the path it takes from the mound. Ben looks at me in complete disbelief, not sure what he can do.

I call a timeout.

I wave Ben over towards me. We meet halfway between the dugout and home plate. The opposing coach is aggravated that I called time during this downpour, but I don't care, I'm trying to find a way to explain to my batter what to do.

As the rain is pouring down on me, I am barely able to keep my eyes open. I tell Ben in a loud manner, "There's nothing we can do about the weather, and this pitcher is throwing his fastballs because he can't control anything else at this point. Expect nothing else but a fastball. Just go up there and swing the hardest you've ever done. Don't let a pitch go by. Even though we can barely see the pitches, even if the pitch is out of the strike zone, the umpire will still call a strike because they want this game to end, but they also want it to be an official game."

"Just go up there and once you see the ball leave the pitchers' hand, estimate where it will be and then swing your life away. I rather you go down swinging instead of having them call the strikes on you. I won't be upset if you strike out swinging, that's the only thing we can do, swing and swing your life away."

As Ben is going back to the plate, he knows what he has to do, it's his only option.

As I watch the pitcher get into his windup, Ben starts to anticipate the location of the ball. The pitcher releases the ball; I lose the ball in the middle of the downpour. Watching to see what Ben is going to do, I focus my attention on him to see if I can tell what's going on.

Suddenly we hear the crack of the bat, but I cannot see where the ball may be. I look over to the one person who I know can see it.

Ben starts to jump ecstatically, and it seems like he hit it hard enough to be a homerun.

Ben is running the bases as fast as he can, unsure if the rain will slow the ball down from traveling the distance. He wants to make sure he can get to the farthest base possible just in case. I look over to the 2nd base umpire running deep into center field; fading quickly the further he goes into the rain.

From afar I see his hand go up, but I can't tell what sign he is displaying.

I watch Ben's emotions.

He slows down and starts trotting through all the bases. The ball is long gone, all the kids rush to home plate to celebrate the game-tying homerun.

Nobody has any idea how far the ball really went except the umpire and maybe the center fielder. Now with the game tied, I'm not sure what the umpires have planned for the remainder of this game. After Ben's homerun, Andover retires the next two batters.

After the half inning is over, the opposing coach and I meet up with the umpires to try and make sense of what to do next. The rain is still coming down aggressively. Talks about ending the game have now begun. The Andover coach is adamant that we continue this half inning, with the weather already postponing games earlier this round, Andover needs to win this game.

62

I'm pretty frank with the umpires and the opposing coach. "After this half inning, it's an official game. One of two things can happen: Andover scores the winning run, or the game ends in a tie. At this point, we just have to focus on the safety of the kids. If you think they are in extreme danger, then the game should be postponed. We shouldn't be standing here since the field conditions are getting worse. If you think they aren't that bad, then we should play, but if we wait any longer then we will have no other choice. Let's get this half inning going, and go from there."

The umpires say, "Both teams can play in this weather, and if the field does get progressively worse, we will suspend it. We'll take it out by out."

Both the opposing coach and I agree; we head back to our respected dugouts. We leave Lenny in to pitch the 4th inning because we want him to consistently pitch his fastball down the middle. We know it will be hard for Andover to keep up with the pitches, and if they do, we strongly believe it won't go too far.

Lenny pitches a 1-2-3 inning.

At the end of the inning, the umpires call the game a 4 – 4 tie. Surprised that the game ended in a tie, the players have no idea if we made it into the trophy weekend or not, and to be honest, I didn't calculate a tie in the thought process either.

I just tell them that we will know more when we play our next game in two days. I just want everyone to get into a vehicle to go home and dry off. I approach Lisa in her SUV as the rain is pouring down.

"Did you see Ben's homerun?"

She looks at me as if I just said something stupid. She condescendingly responds, "I would never miss any of his homeruns, I saw it all the way through. It's one of the longest homeruns, if not the longest, that I've ever seen him hit."

I respond, "I did tell him to swing his bat harder than he has ever done before. It's quite evident he listened to me on this one."

"Aren't you cold standing in the rain?"

"It's only water, plus I've been in it the past couple of hours unlike you staying warm in your SUV."

Ben is able to get his homerun ball that makes us tie the game. I look over to him in the passenger seat.

"You did awesome Ben. That was one incredible homerun."

"Thanks Coach, I'm excited that I was able to get my homerun ball!"

After coming back home, I go to the website and start to figure out the scenarios that could happen. I realize that with the outcomes of the other games, we clinched a spot for the trophy weekend.

The worst we can finish is fourth. We receive one point towards our total for tying the game. We have one more game to play before the playoffs, and if we win, we can be one of the top two seeds. The players still don't know at this point that we have made it into the playoffs. I won't tell them until I have to.

Prior to the start of our last game this round, every player on the team knew that we made it to the trophy weekend. As the team gathered together, I had one more pre-game speech before the trophy weekend would begin.

"I'm sure everyone knows by now that we made it to the trophy weekend, and that is an accomplishment to be proud of. We must focus on this game. We need to make sure we play well from beginning to end. We are all proud of the way this team has played this round. This is exactly what we were talking about in the beginning of the summer. We are almost there. This game is just as important, if not the most important one; to make sure we can play flawless baseball during the trophy weekend. Just like in games before, stay focused. Mentally prepare yourself for any scenario that could happen. Also, have fun doing it. Let's go out there and continue to play as a team and always be there for one another. Let's show everyone that is here at this game that we are ready for the trophy weekend!"

We beat Woburn in the final game of the round 10 – 2. It was a solid performance in all aspects of the game. We gathered all the players after the game to conduct our normal routine postgame speech.

"We are all proud of the way this team has performed this round, this is what we expected. We knew the talent that this team has and it had finally come together. We aren't done with this season just yet; we have more games to play. This Saturday, our first matchup is against East Cambridge. We will meet together on Saturday at two, practice for about a half hour and then head to East Cambridge."

Their field happens to be designated the neutral field for all the games during the trophy weekend.

Framingham is the 1st seed. We are the 2nd seed, East Cambridge and Burlington 3rd and 4th respectively.

The confidence of this team grows steadily from game to game. This team is always humble and well aware that our practices are all for good reasons. They have grasped the thought that practice makes perfect and that we can't make any mental mistakes if we want to make it to the Championship game. This is what we play for, every team, in every division, fighting for this position. The most important part is to always stay focused on the now, and worry about the later when it arrives.

We have just one day off before the big weekend. I tell the team there will be no practice on Friday. I tell them to go home, relax, and have some fun.

After we finish the post-game meeting with the team, Aaron and I are left on the field. I turn to him and tell him, "I'm really proud of this team. The way this league went about having this team constructed aside, I'm excited for this team. We are the underdogs and no one expects rookie summer coaches to make it to the trophy weekend. This is just evidence that when a team can work together and have fun doing so, everything comes together regardless of the talent."

"To be honest Frank, I've been in many summer league rounds as a player, and I've never seen so many kids enjoy playing in the summer as I see on this team. You took winning out of the picture and somehow focused on having fun. You never yell at the kids, which I've seen many coaches do. Their failures you turn into positives. I don't know how you're doing it, but you're building a successful team regardless of what the outcome may be. You've gotten them this far and no one expected that. Not the team that was handed down to us."

"It's just the way I learned from my minor league coach, Aaron. It's something I can share with the rest of the world by being able to coach with what I was taught. I look at it as returning a favor. This is something every coach should focus on."

Later that day, I found out that the B team did not make it to trophy weekend. I found it amusing. All that hard work to gather the best players, to keep them off the A team to make the B team even better ultimately failed.

I never got the chance to see Jerry and Mr. Loney coach a game; our games were played on the same day but on different fields. From what I overheard, there were a lot of players who thought too highly of themselves. It was never a team effort.

This is exactly what I try to prevent as a coach. The team with the better talent lost. The team with the better sportsmanship and team effort has a chance to win. This was just proof that if you coach a team as a unit, anything can happen. We might not win, but at least we can say we have a chance.

CHAPTER TWELVE

July 26, 2008, it's a mild summer sunny afternoon for the first day of the trophy weekend. We have been scheduled for the last game of the day at 4:00pm.

As we arrive, the field that we have been assigned to is currently occupied by a game that was scheduled before us.

Adjacent from our field, the Burlington and Framingham game is going on. As the players are arriving for the game, they head to the warm up area to use the batting cages. Aaron and Jack take the players to the area to warm them up.

Considering we have a while before we play, I decide to watch the matchup between Framingham and Burlington. To my surprise, Framingham has decided to hold their ace for tomorrow's game. Burlington is pitching their ace. When I arrived midway through the third inning, I asked a parent for the score of the game. Framingham currently holds a slim lead, $1 - 0$. At that time, the game playing on our field has just ended.

I gather all of our players and coaches to let them know that it's time to get ready to go onto the field. I have to prepare the lineup which is due within the next fifteen minutes.

We have appointed Lenny our starting pitcher for this game. Lenny has showed us that he is slightly better than Ben. Ben is disappointed that he isn't starting the game.

I approach him and say, "Ben, I understand you want to contribute to this team with your pitching, trust me, you're a great pitcher. Without you, we wouldn't be in this position. We wouldn't be the second ranked team. I ask you to trust us in this situation. I know how East Cambridge reacts to certain pitches. They are a better off-speed hitting team, and your strength is off-speed. This is a great team, and from what I've learned, they have a hard time catching up to the fastball. That is why we have elected Lenny to start."

"Because East Cambridge has a hard time catching up to fastballs, we are going to need you at second base because we expect a lot of plays heading in that direction. You are one of the best defensive players we have in the infield; that is why we need you to play second instead of shortstop today."

Every coach needs to understand in order to build confidence in any player, one must focus on the positives that player has. Every player has strengths, and it's up to the coach to stress them out to that player. It's the only way for the player to understand their contributions to the team.

As the higher ranking team, we are the home team. Lenny starts the game by striking out the side in the first inning. We start the hit brigade in the bottom of the 1st inning; eight batters, six hits, and four runs. After the first inning, we jump to a quick 4 – 0 lead.

Halfway through our game, I happen to notice that the Burlington and Framingham game just ended. It seems that Burlington has upset Framingham. I don't know the score. I just notice that Burlington, in the red jerseys, celebrating the victory.

Some teams assume they can beat any team by saving their ace for the next game, but I've learned that everyone must find a way to win today's game and worry about tomorrow when it arrives. Framingham shot themselves in the foot by electing to save their ace for a game that they will never get to play.

East Cambridge is having a hard time catching up with Lenny's fastball. Lenny has a no-hitter going into the 5th inning with the score 9 – 0.

East Cambridge brings in a substitute to pinch-hit. They want to do anything they can do to get a hit to try and start something. On the first pitch, the batter bunts towards the third base side. The ball, unfortunately for us, was the perfect bunt. The batter reaches safely at first base.

Lenny doesn't show any emotion that the no-hitter was broken up. Just like he has throughout the game, he focuses on the next batter. Although East Cambridge is down by nine runs, they are doing their best to get back into the game. Their next batter swings on the first pitch, and with the crack of the bat, it was a line shot into center field for a two-run homerun.

With Lenny still having an economical pitch count, I call time to go out and talk with him, just to get him relaxed a bit.

"Lenny, you're pitching well, East Cambridge is just able to predict your pitches now. I asked you before the game to consistently throw your fastball and now they have caught up with it, they expect it. They are swinging away at the first pitch, which most of the time are strikes. We have a seven-run lead, a good cushion to work with. I called time just because I want you to start mixing your off-speed pitches in with the fastballs.

Lenny is a quiet kid, barely says anything at all and doesn't show any emotion towards the game. He listens to what I have to say and easily replies with a simple, "Ok."

He has a business like mentality. He does what he has to with no questions asked. I would like him to finish the game. I don't want to use another pitcher today if I don't have to. Whoever pitches today cannot pitch tomorrow.

Lenny starts to mix in his other pitches. It throws East Cambridge off guard. Our players are starting to show excitement as the game nears the end.

At the top of the 6th inning, with each out, the players on the field grow more and more excited. With two outs, the batter swings for the third strike. Every player on the field surrounds Lenny at the mound and celebrates the win. As the manager, I have to temporarily break off the excitement and make sure everyone heads to home plate to shake the other teams' hand.

It only demonstrates great sportsmanship and I preach nothing less than that.

We win the game 9 – 2. Everyone is excited especially after all the hard work that we put into this season. Less than four weeks ago we had so many obstacles to overcome, and now we are guaranteed a trophy. It's always great for the players to leave with a trophy.

First place receives the gold trophy and the runner up is awarded the silver trophy. The first question the team asks us during the post-game speech is, "Who are we playing?"

"It doesn't matter who we are playing. We, as your coaches, will prepare everyone the best way we can to give ourselves the best chance to win. We just ask everyone to keep playing this well and if you do, we'll have a great chance of winning."

All of the coaches, who came to see the game, congratulate us for the victory and then wish us luck for tomorrow.

Mr. Baseball, his first game appearance since he heard about the thirty cents story, takes out thirty cents and gives it to Lisa.

"I want to make sure you get your money back. He's not worth thirty cents." Mr. Baseball starts to laugh.

She shakes her head in disbelief and turns to me and says, "How did I become the scapegoat of your mishap?"

"You are the most vocal parent we have here and if it weren't for you making a big deal about the thirty cents, you probably wouldn't be the laughingstock at this point of the summer, and I thank you for that!"

"I've never seen a team do so well, so quickly. This is quite an amazing run you've put together here." She says.

"You haven't seen anything yet, this is just the beginning." I reply.

"You're a great coach and everyone on the team is excited to be playing for you. I've never seen Ben so excited to play for a team like this before."

I look at her and say, "Lisa this is how I always coach my team. I'm so confident with how this team is playing lately, I will bet you that we will win tomorrow, and if we do, I get to take you out to dinner."

She smirks at me and responds, "I was waiting for you to ask for quite a while now. But what would happen if you were to lose?"

"If we lose, well then, it becomes an option for you."

"I don't think it's going to be an option, I've already made up my mind. I just wanted to see what you would say."

"So it's a date!"

I walk away with a confident smile, knowing that I've just solidified a date with this radiant, stunning woman for tomorrow night after the conclusion of our game.

Aaron notices my unusual skip with my step and says, "You seem quite chirpy."

"Well, I've just orchestrated a date for tomorrow night with Lisa."

"Wow, really. How did that happen?"

"I opened the door to the possibility by betting her that if we win tomorrow night, I get to take her out on a date."

"Not to jinx us or anything like that, but what would happen if we were to lose?"

"It does not matter if we win or lose. She's actually been waiting for me to ask her out. Ever since the thirty cents fiasco occurred, we've been flirting, but I wanted to wait because I didn't want anyone to think that my decisions were biased in favoring Ben. I meticulously waited until I knew when the summer league would be officially over before I would ask Lisa out on a date. Regardless of the outcome of the game, we will be going out tomorrow night; the season will be officially over."

"That's good man. I have to tell Jack when I see him."

It seems like Aaron is more excited than I am. None of the other coaches know that Lisa and I tentatively agreed to go out tomorrow after the game. I didn't want anyone to know at this point. I didn't want anyone to think that there was any favoritism towards Ben. I have asked Aaron not to tell anybody yet, it really isn't any of their business and I don't want anything to be blown out of proportion. I told him to wait until the season is over.

"We need to focus on tomorrow's game. Who should we pitch for tomorrow's game?"

Aaron and I are in a predicament, Lenny can't pitch tomorrow, and with Ben's style of pitching, it follows suit to Burlington's strength. Burlington was the only team that really beat up on Ben's pitching. We played them once before and they beat us 9 – 6. We have an eleven-year old that only pitched with the B team this season. He is allowed to pitch for both the A and B team as long as he is listed as a starter on the B team, and is listed as an alternate on the A team.

With our lack of pitching, we are contemplating starting Mark over Ben just because we know Burlington will remember the game that Ben pitched against them.

I know Burlington's confidence will grow even higher before the game if they know Ben is pitching. With Mark, his fastball is one of the fastest of his age group. But by putting an eleven-year old as a starting pitcher for one of the biggest games, it puts a lot of pressure on him considering Burlington's team consists of all twelve year olds.

Aaron and I go over the pros and cons throughout the night. Still unsure of exactly who we should start, we take a look at Mark's performance and compare it to Ben's performance throughout the two rounds. After remembering the struggles Ben had with Burlington the last time we played them, Aaron and I elect to go with Mark. It's one of the hardest decisions we have to make as a coaching staff, but we know, at this point, that Mark will give us a better chance. Even though in the past, Mark has had trouble in big games, I feel I can help his nerves and get him better prepared for it.

We want to give Burlington something they haven't seen yet, a pitcher that they most likely won't prepare for. From the very beginning, we have to try and throw Burlington off their game.

CHAPTER THIRTEEN

The Championship game has arrived. The forecast predicts rain, but not until later on in the evening. The game starts at two and I have asked everyone to meet at our field first before we head over to East Cambridge at noon.

I want to give Mark some time to adjust to the fact that we have decided to start him for the game. I also want to talk to Ben, because after yesterday's game, he assumes he is going to start this game. He thinks he is the only option left. Jack and Aaron have begun the defense drills, I pull Ben aside.

This is one of those moments any coach hates to tell a kid, but disappointment is a part of life and it's how coaches present it that can make it a better outcome.

"Ben, come over here please."

"Yes coach, what's up?"

"I noticed yesterday that you were pretty excited about today's game."

"Why shouldn't I be? It's a big game."

"I overheard you talking to your mother that you believe you are pitching this game."

"Well yeah, who else is there? That's the reason why you were talking to my mother for so long after the game…right?"

Doing my best to avoid the reason why I was actually talking to Ben's mother as long as I did, I quickly remind him of the last time we played Burlington.

"Do you remember the last time we played Burlington?"

"Yes, I do. They killed us and I didn't pitch that well."

"Although you gave it your best and we commend you for your effort during that game, it was a tough game. But this time we have to pitch someone else. We have a few reasons why. If Burlington knows you're starting this game, they'll remember the last game you pitched against them. This now becomes a mind game Ben. In order to give us the best chance, we must make sure they are up against something they have never seen before."

"All the games that we've played this season, they can look up and see how you pitched, how Lenny pitched, and the other pitchers we've used this season. What they won't look at is how a pitcher performed that was on the B team. This is a very well-organized team and so are we. They are expecting you to pitch this game. They believe you're the only option we have left. Once they see who is pitching today, they won't know what to do. That's how we have to start the game, with them confused in the very beginning."

"Trust me, this isn't easy for me to do, but it is the right decision. As you've noticed, we put this team in the best position to win games. With that being said Ben, please understand what we are doing, and if you ever become a coach, you will understand. There's still a possibility we may need you to come in to pitch relief, but we won't know that until we see how the game progresses."

Disappointed, he looks at me and asks, "Who is pitching?"

"We have decided to pitch Mark in today's game. You must understand that without you Ben, we wouldn't be in this position. Without you hitting that game tying home run against Andover in the pouring rain, we wouldn't be the home team. We wouldn't be the number two seed, and we might not have won yesterday's game. We could've easily played Framingham or Burlington yesterday but we didn't. Your home run ultimately decided our fate of where we are today. Your home run had the biggest impact of our season, always remember that Ben."

The disappointed look slowly fades; he realizes that he was the one player who changed the fate of this team.

He looks at me and says, "Coach, although I am disappointed that I am not pitching in today's game, we as a team have done well and I know you, as well as the other coaches, are doing the best you can to put this team in the best position to win the game, and that is the most important thing; team effort over individual effort, like it should always be."

His response amazes me. The one thing I have always talked about to this team is that it is always about team effort. If one player understands that, if I can change just one player's thought process like that, I feel I have done well as a coach.

78

"Ben, one thing I can tell you is that you'll be starting at shortstop this game. Just be mentally prepared for that."

"Thanks Coach, where am I batting in the order?"

"I haven't started to think about it yet, but I believe you'll be second in the order, which is your original spot."

I had expected nothing but disappointment. I was shocked by his surprisingly calm response.

At this point, I call Mark over.

"Yes coach?"

"We have decided to appoint you as the starter for today's game."

"Wow, really?!"

"The one thing I ask you to do is stay with your fastballs until I tell you to throw your off-speed pitches. You haven't faced this team yet, as your coach I ask you to listen to what I have to say about this team and if you do, we'll have a great chance of winning."

"You want me to stick with just my fastballs?"

"Yes. Just stay calm and listen to me when I tell you what to pitch and where to pitch them. Go warm up with Coach Aaron and I'll talk to you again before the game."

I'm leaning over the fence watching the fielding drills Jack is conducting when Lisa approaches me and says, "I've never seen Ben so excited about not pitching. Usually he pouts when he doesn't get his way. He swore up and down last night that he was really excited to pitch today's game and when he received the news that he wasn't, you still found a way to make him excited. How did you do it?"

I respond, "I just know the right things to say. I know how to make light of a situation by instilling a confidence booster at the end of the conversation. You always want to end a disappointing conversation with an uplifting reminder of why that person is important."

"Frank, Ben kept asking me last night after the game if you told me that he was pitching today, as hard as it was for me to answer that question, all I could say is that we were just talking. He doesn't suspect anything of what we have planned for tonight. I made plans with his grandfather to pick him up after the game so he can stay with him a few days."

"Ok, sounds great."

As we get the equipment over to our bench, I can smell cigarette smoke. I can't stand the smell of cigarettes. I look all over the place and I say, "Who's smoking a cigarette? I can smell it but I don't see anyone smoking."

Lisa is right next to me and I ask her, "Do you see anyone smoking a cigarette?"

"No, I don't. Is it a problem?"

"I understand people smoke but I try to stay away from it, it makes me sick from time to time."

I never did find out who was smoking, but the smell of the smoke had gone away.

I have to make sure Mark is ready for the game.

"Mark, are you ready?"

"Yes, Coach. I am ready."

"You'll do great! Just take your time between pitches. You control the game and I want to make sure you don't rush any of your throws."

With Burlington pitching their ace yesterday, their second pitcher is just a slight notch behind him. To our advantage, he pitched against us the last game as well. I learned a few things while he was pitching the last time. I kept notes of what he pitched during certain counts. I just had to verify within the first two innings whether or not he was sticking to his normal routine.

Burlington was quite surprised that Mark was pitching this game. They had to verify that Mark was on the roster. The roster has to be set before the round begins. It was easily verified by not only the website where the rosters are posted, but also by the Commissioner of the summer league who is at every trophy weekend just in case there are any problems that may arise.

Burlington's game plan was thrown a curve ball; they expected Ben, but now Mark is pitching and they have no idea what to expect. This is exactly what I anticipated. Everything seems to go according to our plan. I knew it was going to be a tough game, and with Burlington confused as to why I am starting Mark, it makes the game even more interesting.

During the first two innings it was a stalemate, both teams scattered a few hits but nothing more than that. After two innings the game is tied $0 - 0$. After watching Burlington's pitcher and his patterns, I can anticipate most of his pitches.

At the bottom of the 3rd inning, I gather the team in the dugout.

"Everyone, do not swing at the first pitch. I want you to wait for the first strike. Once the pitcher falls behind the count, he stays with his fastball. His curveball is rarely used but when it is, it's on the obvious 1 – 2 count or the first pitch with no runners on base. This is why I am asking all of you to wait for the first pitch to go by. Once he throws the first pitch and if it's a ball, he'll focus strictly on his fastball. I want him to throw a lot of pitches.

The first two runners reached base via the walk.

Mark comes up to the plate. The first pitch was a ball. Keeping in mind what I had told him, Mark looks over to me. I say, "If it looks good, swing away."

With the anticipation of it being a fastball, Mark didn't want any strikes to go by him. On the very next pitch, with the sound of the bat, everyone immediately knew the ball was gone. It was a monster three-run homerun in center field.

The ball left in a hurry. We jumped to 3 – 0 lead.

That is all we would get in the inning.

The bottom of the 4th inning, Burlington decides to pull their pitcher; their starter has thrown close to one-hundred pitches and everyone could sense the fatigue that was setting in. They decide to throw a pitcher who can efficiently throw strikes, but his velocity isn't up to par with most of the pitchers in the league.

In the bottom of the 4th inning, we were able to score another run to make it 4 to 1.

During the top of the 5th inning Burlington storms right back.

All of a sudden the score becomes 4 – 3.

I call a timeout and head out to talk with Mark.

"How are you feeling?"

"I feel a little tired but I want to finish this inning."

"Your pitch count is getting up there. I'll give you one more batter. If you want to stay in the game, you have to get this batter out."

"Ok, I'll get him."

With runners on 1st and 2nd and two outs, I give him the benefit of the doubt.

Mark walks the next batter.

I call time again and walk out to the mound to make the switch. As I am making my way to the mound, I have no idea who I want to pitch. With the bases loaded, I didn't want to put Ben in this situation, biased or not, I just didn't want to put him in that predicament.

I call over to DeAndre from left field and bring him in to pitch. He's a solid pitcher, he can be wild but he is intimidating to other batters with his height and velocity.

I want someone who Burlington hasn't seen yet. DeAndre is the tallest player on the team; when he's on, he has a devastating fastball. His warm up throws were right down the middle.

The first pitch DeAndre throws to the batter is high and inside but the batter swings at it. The opposing coach prior to the batter going to the plate must have told him to swing at the first pitch because he saw DeAndre's pitches go right down the middle. We are fortunate that he swung on that one.

With a full-count, bases loaded, and two outs, the next pitch may decide the outcome of the game. When a game gets this exciting and intense, I start my usual pacing back and forth up and down the baseline. DeAndre starts his wind-up, the crowd so quiet that even a pin drop can be heard.

The next thing everyone hears is the umpire's voice, "STRIKE 3."

I've never seen the players run off the field so quickly at the end of the inning. We are able to get out of the inning with a one-run lead.

With Burlington just one run away of tying the score, we gather the team together to try and get some insurance runs on the board. They know that the end is near and with three more outs, we can win. I have to make sure that they stay focused.

"We can't think about what can happen, we need to start thinking what can we do now. This is our game to win, but only if you want to win, we have to finish strong. Go out there and make sure Burlington knows that we haven't finished scoring yet. If they want to beat us, they need to pull out all the stops on us." I explain to my team.

We answer their rally right back with one of our own.

Batter after batter had the ability to get a hit off the new pitcher. Burlington doesn't have any other pitchers to use. We are able to get a comfortable lead. We are making a statement to Burlington. If they are going to beat us, they are going to need to score at least five runs in the top of the inning to have a chance.

Burlington could only muster one run at the top of the inning. DeAndre recorded the final out of the game via the strikeout.

All the players on the field and the bench run to the mound and bombard DeAndre. After a few minutes, we line up at the plate. Players shake hands first, the coaches go last.

As the opposing coach and I shake hands, I congratulate him, "Your team played very well. It was a great game."

"Thanks, your team did a tremendous job! Congrats!"

It wasn't easy and I didn't expect it to be. The players deserve this; they played flawlessly the past few games. They did it when it counted the most.

Before the game, I had asked all the players who were on the roster if they could attend. Even though we are restricted to play a maximum of twelve players per game, each player should be present to be awarded a trophy. Every player participated in at least one game during the course of the season and each player was deserving of a trophy.

There were only eighteen player trophies, and we had twenty total players. Both Aaron and Jack gave up their trophy to the players. There was one more trophy, it was the biggest one. It was handed to the manager of the winning team. I'm not one to say it's my trophy, it was our trophy; we won it as a team, always as a team.

The Commissioner of the league presented the Gold trophy to me, as the manager. During the picture the league takes, I want to make sure all of our coaches have a hand on the trophy.

I was unprepared to make a speech of which the Commissioner asked me to do. Usually I am very shy when conducting speeches in front of people I don't know.

After the ceremony, I told everyone that we ordered pizza and that instead of going to a pizza place, the players insisted we go to our field, on the other side of Cambridge to celebrate.

Before we leave the field, Lisa says to me, "Ben's grandfather will be taking him to celebrate with the team and I am heading home, so I can get ready for tonight."

"Ok, let's plan for seven?"

"Yes, that sounds great!"

"Great, I'll call you when I am on my way."

"Ok, I will talk to you then."

I have one last post-game meeting to make with these players. Since we are out of contention for the Tournament of Champions, we decide as a coaching staff not to sign up for the third round and leave on a high note.

"This is the last time that this group will be together in the majors. Some of you will go to Babe Ruth, while the others will focus on other activities. It was a great season and I've never had as much fun coaching as I have this season. You guys deserve this."

All the parents start making their way over to me, one by one.

"Frank, I just want to thank you for such a great season my kid had on your team. It was great to see such a great attitude towards the way you present yourself to them. It's not often that coaches never yell or criticize their players. I never heard you say anything bad about anyone. Again, thank you for the way you coach the game." A parent explains.

They'd never seen such a great group of coaches who focused on sportsmanship and where winning wasn't a priority. Winning just comes natural once everyone starts having fun and that's what this season was about. Everyone noticed that when you're having fun, winning follows suit.

After spending an hour celebrating, I look at my watch and notice that I have to leave. I have to pick up Lisa at seven o'clock. I have to make sure I'm on time. I'm never late for anything. I head home to take a quick shower so I can clean up before I pick up Lisa at her house.

CHAPTER FOURTEEN

I pull up to Lisa's house ten minutes before seven. I call her letting her know I'm outside, I don't know which apartment is hers.

She says she will be right out.

Forty minutes later she finally comes strolling out of the house.

"I'm sorry for running so late, but I couldn't decide what to wear."

She has a black and white silk dress on. I am completely stunned on how she looks.

"You are simply beautiful." I'm trying to stop my mouth from dropping so low of complete amazement.

I'm used to waiting for women; it's something I've gotten accustomed to throughout the years. Men are always waiting for women to get ready, that's nothing new these days. Just like any gentleman should, I open the door for her.

We are having dinner at Frank's Steakhouse in Cambridge on Massachusetts Avenue. I open the restaurant door for her; I pull out her chair, she sits down, and then I push her closer to the table.

The waitress comes over to us.

"What would you like to drink?"

I look right at Lisa, "What do you usually drink with dinner when you go out with your friends?"

"I usually get a strawberry daiquiri."

"We might as well celebrate the victory with a drink!"

I turn to the waitress, "She'll have a strawberry daiquiri…"

Lisa chimes in, putting her hand forward making a circle motion with her finger, "With salt on the rim please."

I'll have a Bud Light, draft please.

As the drinks arrive, she proposes a toast, "This is for having an excellent baseball season and winning the Gold trophy!"

As we put our drinks together, some of her strawberry daiquiri falls into my beer. Before she can say anything, I reassure her, "Don't worry about it; it just adds a little flavor."

Lisa looks me in the eyes, her feet rubbing against my legs.

"How long have you been coaching?"

"I just finished my fifth year. My first three years I was an assistant in the minor leagues. But this is my second year as the manager of the major Giants."

"You've been coaching for five years? How old are you?"

89

"I just turned twenty-seven last week."

She looks at me and states, "I just had a birthday two weeks ago! I'm ten years older than you."

"Wow! You don't look any older than thirty!"

"I guess we are also celebrating our birthdays!" I pull my glass up for another toast, "Happy birthday to the both of us!"

"I won't spill my drink in yours this time, I swear."

She carefully and slowly puts up her glass next to mine and ever-so slightly we tap our glasses together.

Lisa orders the prime rib and I order the Rib-eye steak.

"Frank you did a great job coaching the kids and it is the most fun that my son has ever had playing baseball. I've never had so much fun in a matter of weeks. The thirty cents was by far the funniest thing I've ever encountered."

"I'm glad you had just as much fun as Ben did. See how easy it is to have fun. The littlest things create the best laughs."

"Frank, looking back on how Ben has performed in past years, it's quite amazing how well he's doing. It has been hard for Ben to play in Central Cambridge. When Ben was seven, he wasn't a very skilled baseball player. It was hard to place him on a team in the beginning. I didn't get a call after the first tryouts, or the second tryouts. I felt bad for him. I knew he had trouble catching and hitting the ball, but I just wanted someone to give him a chance. He was eventually drafted late in the spring. He was the very last kid drafted in the minors. Even in the majors, Ben again went late in the draft. However, every time he is given a chance to prove himself, he shines."

Throughout the entire night she's playing footsies with me, slowly moving her feet up and down on my leg. She keeps saying my name during dinner. She must have said it about twenty times; I knew that was a telling sign. I look over at the clock and notice that it's slightly past eleven. Time had flown by very fast and before we knew it, it was getting late. We talked for four hours, enjoying one another's company a great deal.

We leave Frank's Steakhouse and I, like a gentleman, take care of the bill and give the waitress a 25% tip.

I open the car door for her, wait for her to sit down and get comfortable in her seat and then quietly shut the door.

As I am driving, Lisa grabs my right hand and places our palms together.

"I had a great time at dinner this evening. You are really funny."

"Don't tell my friends that, they won't believe you."

"What do you mean? Your friends don't think you're funny?"

"No one thinks I'm funny. Everyone thinks I'm too serious, but they just don't understand my sense of humor and you, on our first date, understood it. That doesn't happen often."

"I thought you were hilarious. You have a great sense of humor!"

I park my car, turn to Lisa and say, "Don't get out yet."

Her street is a one way street; I can park on either side. There is a spot on the left side of the street right across from her apartment. I get out of my car first and go around to her door making sure no vehicles are coming and assist her in getting out of my vehicle, just like any gentleman should.

I walk her back to her front door. She looks at me and says, "I really enjoyed tonight. I can't remember the last time anyone opened the car door for me."

She opens her front door and turns back towards me.

"It has been a very long time since anyone has treated me like this. It was one of the best nights I've had in while."

"I had a great time as well--"

Before I can even finish my sentence, she grabs my shirt by the collar, pulls me forward and our lips come together. As we place our hands on one another's face, tilting our heads slowly caressing one another's cheeks, she pushes me back.

"I shouldn't be doing this." She adds.

"You don't have to."

As I take a few steps back.

I say, "I won't do anything you don't want me to."

I start to turn around to go back to my car.

She steps towards me, grabs my arm from behind, turns me around and pulls me closer to her once again, but this time she puts her arm over my left shoulder. She then puts her left hand on the back of my head and pulls me close to her once more; we put our heads closer in an enticing motion. Our bodies pull one another in the hallway. We are right in front of another door that must lead into her apartment. As her back is facing the door, she somehow finds a way to use her right hand and unlock the door from behind her back. I don't how she did it, but it was amazing.

Just before she pulls me into the house, she stops for the second time.

"I really shouldn't be doing this. I don't know what has gotten into me."

Not saying a word, I lean into her and I give her a kiss on the lips.

"It's not a problem, I understand. I will call you---"

Without being able to finish my sentence, she pulls me with this great rush of intensity from the shoulders. She turns me so that I am completely facing her, pulls my arms closer and our lips connect in an aggressive manner. Her hand is firmly placed on the back of my head, her teeth biting my lip.

We slowly make our way into her apartment. Right as we get inside, our bodies fall onto her couch. The couch is the closest thing, and that is all that we need.

Our shirts quickly fly off our bodies, in a matter of seconds every piece of clothing is being thrown all over the place. The tender but subtle bite marks I apply to her body set off an enticing moan; at that moment her fingers slowly scratch downward on my back.

Not another word is spoken for hours; sounds, but no words.

After a few hours in her apartment, I lean towards her and give her a kiss on the lips.

As I slowly get dressed, she puts her arm on my shoulder as leverage to lift her body up and then she whispers, "Thanks for such a great night" as she nibbles on my ear.

I put my hand on her face, slowly sliding it down. I give her another kiss on the lips and I say with satisfaction, "It was my pleasure."

I quietly shut the door behind me and I think to myself, I did not expect this night to finish as it did. It was the first time that I sensed something different. I wasn't quite sure what it was, but this night was definitely unusual for my standards.

One thing I do know, Lisa is an animal.

CHAPTER FIFTEEN

I want to wait a couple of days before I call Lisa. I like to take things slow and to get to know someone before I get too heavily involved. On the other hand, the other night was by no means taking it slow.

Two days pass and I finally decide to call her.

"Hello?"

"Hello Lisa, how are you?"

"I didn't think you were going to call me. I thought we had a great time the other night."

I think to myself, I never know whether I should call the next day or wait a couple of days. Everybody tells me different things. It seems like I can never pin point when the right time to call a woman again after the first date.

"I had a great time too! I just waited because I was trying to figure out if you wanted me to call you or not. That's why I was waiting, I didn't want to seem like I wanted to rush into anything."

She chuckles, "So the other night was just a casual night out for you?"

I'm laughing hysterically.

"Honestly not at all. I don't have sex on the first date."

"So, are you saying I'm easy?"

I'm lost for words. Everything I say she finds something to come back with.

"That's it, I quit. You win. Whatever you say, you're right."

"Wow, you're a quick learner."

"Yeah, I know when to stop before I dig myself into a bigger hole. I'm used to it from all my friends these past years. I know when to quit."

After talking on the phone for hours, the question finally arises.

"When are we going out again?" She asks.

"Are you free Friday night?"

"Yes, I am."

"I can pick you up at five. Is that ok?"

"Yes, that sounds great!"

I pull up to her apartment fifteen minutes before five. I'm always early. Five o'clock has come and gone and to no surprise, she comes strolling out a half hour later.

As I open her car door, I say to her, "Ten minutes faster this time. You're getting better at not being too late." As I half-smile at her, I quickly add that I'm only kidding.

"There's that sense of humor of yours. Where are we going?"

"I have decided that since it's nice out, we are going gallivanting on the beach. Enjoy the sunset, walk across the sand, and just enjoy the scenery. Something that's peaceful, yet for me, always enjoyable. If not, we can do something else."

"The beach sounds like a great idea! I haven't been to a beach since Ben was a little boy. I enjoy the water, the sounds of the waves. It's fine by me."

"You can decide where we are going to eat afterwards."

"Oh, I don't know about that. I'm not good at making decisions."

"That's the easiest decision you can make. When the time comes, just pick a place where you like to eat. It doesn't matter where. Well, as long as it's not Burger King or McDonalds. I'm thinking more of a real-dine in restaurant."

"We'll go to Wendy's!"

She starts to laugh, and notes, "You're not the only one with a sense of humor around here!"

I chuckle even though I didn't think it was that funny.

We park across the street from Revere Beach.

We start to walk down the beach front. I'm making sure I walk on the side closer to the street, to lessen any danger that may come from the streets. This is another common gentleman etiquette everyone should be aware of.

Ten steps into our walk she grabs my hand and entwines our fingers together, holding hands during our walk. We walk what must've seemed about a mile, I look over to her and ask, "Would you like to sit down?"

"Yes please, my feet are starting to bother me. That is if you don't mind?"

"No, not at all, I did recommend it."

It was pretty romantic in my eyes. I'll admit I can be a hopeless romantic at times. I have a great heart but I also like candlelight dinners, walking on the beach, and going to fancy restaurants when possible. Watching the sunset, seeing the orange-reddish color the sky turns in the middle of the summer, right before dusk; watching the waves crash into one another, hearing the sound of the water coming up to shore and the seagulls adding their voices; it is a peaceful meditating way to self-preserve ones soul.

We take a seat on the beach wall. After just a few minutes Lisa starts the conversation.

"Frank, there's something I have to tell you."

"Yes Lisa, what is it?"

"When Ben was five years old, he asked me if he could have a brother. I tried to tell him that I couldn't but he didn't understand why. I can't have any more children. Ben is all I have and I wish I could have more children of my own. I had to tell you now because I did not want you to be disappointed if this went any further. I wanted to make sure I told you up front because I felt it was something that you should know. If it's something you want, you won't be able to have any if you're with me. If you want to, you can leave now."

I pause for a couple of seconds; it feels like a scene from a movie. I then take her hand and look up at her.

"Lisa, children of my own is the least of my concerns. If this goes any further, it's because our love for one another has grown, and at that point it would be the strongest thing, and more importantly, all anyone ever truly needs; is someone to love."

"I just want to make sure that you know now that I can't have any more children and I wish that I could, but Ben will be my only child. I had to tell you."

I take her hand, turn her face towards me and say, "We shouldn't even be thinking about that right now, and if by any means we fall in love with one another, our love can supersede any other complication that may arise during the relationship. If I love you, it's because of who you are, and nothing else can stop such a feeling."

After that, she breathes a sigh of relief.

"I just wanted to make sure that you are aware of the situation, that if you want any children of your own, it won't be with me. I would've been ok with you leaving."

"Lisa, that is not even on my mind. I thank you for being straight-forward with me but that's not something I'm concerned about."

"Ben doesn't have a relationship with his father. I kicked him out of the house when he was very young. Ben's father was very abusive to me and he was heavily into drugs and alcohol. I was able to take the abuse from Ben's father, but once he hit Ben, I had enough. I took out a restraining order on him. There are quite a few men that I have a restraining order on, but that's another story for another time. There are many times he lurks the streets nearby where we live. He just happens to live in our neighborhood and I try my best to protect Ben from him.

Ben has never had a male influence in his life to talk to or just someone to guide him. All the things that fathers and sons do: go to the movies, bowling, and going to baseball games at Fenway Park etc. He has never had that bond with anyone. I know I can only be the mother, and I wish Ben had someone he could talk to. I know I can't give him that aspect in life, but I will try as best as I can."

I know how Ben feels. My parents divorced when I was four years old. I have two younger brothers. One of which is eleven months younger than me and another one that is nine years younger; he has a different father.

Once my mother and father divorced, as the eldest, I was indirectly given a responsibility; to take care of the family as best as I could. I was always there for everyone regardless of the good or bad times, and I will always be there for my family. Growing up around me, all the friends that I had, their parents were together. They would all go on family trips and enjoy family functions. Growing up, I never enjoyed such a thing. I idolized families because in the end, that's what I wanted our family to be like, and that's what I want my family, when I have one, to be like.

As a family, we never had the opportunity to take family trips. As we were growing up, my mother raised the three of us by herself. She didn't have time to get a job. My mother had to raise us day in and day out. We had to rely on child support and government assistance. That still wasn't enough. There would be times we didn't have electricity, gas, or heat, but we had food on the table and we were able to survive.

Living without a father in the household is something that I'm familiar with. I know how Ben feels without having a male influence present every day.

I sit next to Lisa, with her head on my shoulder and the wind blowing her hair, she is starting to get cold; her shivering legs shake my body completely.

After gazing into the sun, watching the few minutes that it has left before it would say goodbye for the night, Lisa turns to me and says, "Frank, I have something a little more important to speak about now. Right now, Ben is all I have but I'm afraid that I won't be there for him."

"What do you mean?"

"Well, it's been a few months now, but I have been diagnosed with a brain tumor."

I'm a little shocked by this revelation.

"What kind of tumor?"

"It's malignant."

"How long did they say you have?"

"I'm not sure, months, maybe a year if I'm lucky."

"I can be there for you if you want me to be there for you. We can only take one day at a time and it doesn't bother me one bit."

"Are you sure?"

"Lisa, I'm glad you were upfront with me and because you did that, it shows that you care about us being together. Being

101

honest and trustworthy is a great start in building a strong foundation for a relationship."

"Please do not say anything to Ben or anybody else. Nobody knows about my health, and I don't want anyone else to know. I want to try and figure this out on my own, but I wanted to let you know so I don't scare you away. But if you want to, you can leave now, I would understand."

"If there is anything you need me to do, just let me know. I'll do the best I can."

Lisa doesn't say another word after that. She just lays her head on my shoulder as we are watching the sunset. A few minutes later, she lifts her head towards mine and we join our lips together.

"Can we leave now? I'm starting to get cold."

"Yes, we can leave."

As we walk back to the car, we are holding hands and it seems she feels at ease about telling me what she is going through. It's not easy to tell someone that you're dying. I can only imagine that thought process. At least she has someone to be there for her when the time comes. We are holding hands and talking about everything. Well, mostly Ben, which is something I expect. Ben is everything to her.

"I gave you plenty of time to decide what restaurant, have you decided where we are going for dinner?"

"Ah shucks, I was hoping you would forget that I had to decide where to go to eat."

"I didn't forget that part. Do you have something in mind?"

"Yes, I have something in mind. Just drive towards Target in Somerville. It is a few blocks from there."

We pull up in front of La Hacienda; it's practically in the middle of nowhere. I never knew of this place. I was born and raised around this area.

"Why did you pick this place?"

"I picked this place because it's in the middle of nowhere, it is quiet and there is always a table."

It's obvious that she hates waiting. I wonder if she realizes how often I wait for her. I think it's funny; I will wait to say it another time.

As we are about to sit down, a person comes up to Lisa. She knows her. After they have a brief conversation, she sits down distraught.

"She's my aunt. I haven't seen her in a very long time. I do not talk to them anymore. When I was younger, I had to get away from my family. It's another story for another day, but right now I just want to enjoy dinner."

I can tell that it reminded her of her past and she didn't want to go back there. At that point I know she feels uncomfortable, so I change the subject to the one thing she loves to talk about: Ben.

"So have you talked to Ben about us yet?"

She looks at me and starts to laugh.

"What's so funny?"

"I did mention you to Ben and he was so funny about it. I asked him, what would you think if I went out with Coach Frank?

His reply was simply hilarious. He said, 'Doesn't he have to call you first?'"

We both laugh hysterically.

"Obviously you told him about the story when I lost your number. That is funny."

As the night is ending, I ask Lisa if it would be possible to take Ben out to play baseball sometime this week. I know the All-Star game and Babe Ruth tryouts are around the corner, I'm sure he'll want to practice for that.

"He loves to play and I am sure he would enjoy it. That's his passion. I'm sure he would rather play with you than his own mother. He'll love it."

"Great, sounds like a plan."

As I am walking her to the front door, I give her a kiss on the lips.

"You know we have plenty of time before Ben comes home. You can come in if you'd like."

"Sure, why not. I don't have any plans."

I know exactly what she is hinting towards. So what, if the opportunity arises, why not take advantage of it. It's not like it's our first date, it went so well the first time.

After a few hours and after a couple of times, Lisa's phone rings.

It's Ben. He's on his way home. He's in Nahant, we have about thirty minutes.

I'm in complete disbelief that she wants to go again. Damn, the woman is a beast in so many ways. I'm young, I can handle it. Clearly Lisa is a different shade of grey that I've never experienced before.

We finish literally five minutes before Ben comes home. Lisa and I go to the couch; she puts on the TV as if nothing ever happened.

It was perfect timing.

Lisa opens the door for Ben and I am sitting on the couch.

"Hey Coach, how's it going?"

"Not bad, how are you Ben?"

"Good, good."

Lisa chimes in, "Ben if you want to, Frank said you two can play baseball on Tuesday."

"Of course I do Ma, that's almost a stupid question. I never turn down playing sports."

"Yeah I know, plus you'll have someone who won't throw like a girl."

I stay for an hour after Ben arrives home.

"I have to go home and get up for work in the morning."

I give Lisa a kiss on the lips.

"I will talk to you later."

I turn to Ben and say, "I'll see you Tuesday at three o'clock at my field."

CHAPTER SIXTEEN

I arrive at the park a half-hour early. It starts to rain, it is only a light drizzle.

Lisa calls me. "Are the two of you still going to be playing in the rain?"

"Of course we are it's only a little water."

"You guys are insane."

Lisa and Ben arrive at the field thirty minutes late. I look at Ben. He gives me a look that says 'we just lost thirty minutes of baseball time because she had to do her hair.'

"It's not your fault Ben. Women take forever to get ready. You'll get used to it when you're older."

We take out the baseball equipment, and as we are heading on the field, it starts to pour. We rush back into the dugout to wait for the rain to go away.

"Do you think I'll make Babe Ruth?"

"Of course Ben, you're a great ball player. You are one of the best baseball players in the city. You just have to be confident in yourself."

"But what if I don't make it?"

"Ben, the best advice I have for you at this point is to remember this: I've been coaching for five years now and I know talent when I see it. Sometimes though, talent isn't enough. It's the heart, the fight in one's heart to keep getting better. You have the talent, that's quite evident. The fight in your heart keeps getting stronger. Take a look back when you first started. You haven't taken a step backward, you've always gotten better. If you keep fighting to get better, I guarantee you that you'll do well. I can promise that you'll make Babe Ruth. I don't promise often but when I do, I make sure I fulfill my promises."

"Ben, my draft is coming up in a few weeks and I have the second pick. Earlier this year I thought I knew who I wanted to pick. But as the season progressed, I just don't know who I want. It's a 50/50 chance of who I'm going to pick. Everybody thinks I'm picking Juan, who has great power and speed. He throws his fastball at blazing speeds, but he can be wild when he pitches. The other pick is Eddie, he has a great baseball mind, and he's a great pitcher and a great hitter. It is an overall tie. I don't know who I'm going to pick."

"What makes you think both will be available to choose from since you have the second pick in the draft?" Ben asks.

"Rodney has the first pick and I'm pretty sure he's drafting a kid he coached in the minor leagues a year ago. Plus this player has two younger brothers. Rodney likes to apply the brother rule to make sure they will play for his team when they are old enough for the majors. Rodney is predictable for his first pick in this draft.

I think Eddie is a good ball player and a great team player. Juan is also a good ball player, but his head is not in the game very much."

"Who else are you going to choose?"

"I will have picks ten and eleven after my first one. If it works out, I will pick Andre and Jim. Both players are from the Diamondbacks; the team I coached in the minors. Andre is a big kid, he has a lot of potential for power, and if I can make him into a pitcher, he will be very intimidating. Jim is an all-around solid player. He can pitch, field, and hit. He doesn't have power but he has heart. He's a natural team leader. We need that on the Giants. Like I told you Ben, Jim has the fight in his heart and it shows day in and day out with him. I strongly believe he'll be a great ball player because of that."

"I believe these two players will do well. Only time will tell. I'm confident that both Andre and Jim will be available, but my first pick in the draft is the hardest."

"Just go with what you believe is right, that's what made us win the Gold trophy."

"You're right Ben. I know I'll figure it out and I truly believe both Juan and Eddie are great picks no matter what. It might come down to who I think might be the better player when they are twelve years old. It's a dead heat between the two of them and I know it might not even matter. I would ask Jack and

Aaron for their opinion, but they've made it clear that since I go to all the games and scout the players, they trust my judgment."

The rain starts to diminish.

"Ben do you want to pitch first or would like to hit first?"

"I would like to hit first.

After he hits for a while, I want to physically see all of the pitches he says he has. If he is one of the top two pitchers in his league, there's a good chance he's going to pitch in the Inter-City All-Star tournament in September.

"Ben, you said you've got five pitches?"

"Yes, I do."

"Which one is your best pitch?"

"My curveball is my best pitch, as you witnessed in the summer."

"I want you to throw each pitch to me five times and show me how accurate you are with them."

For the first time, someone focuses on his pitching. Yes, his mother plays catch with him, but now, he is excited that he can actually improve his pitches with someone who has experience.

He didn't throw very much in the summer, so I was unable to see all of his pitches. I know about his lack of control with his fastball, and I had heard about his off-speed stuff, but now, I am witnessing it firsthand and focusing on it with him.

His best pitches are his off-speed ones. This is no surprise to me. I am amazed, not with his control of these pitches, but with his lack of his control with his fastball. Once we get his fastball under control, he will be a great pitcher.

We play baseball for an hour and a half and the rain starts up again. If it weren't for the weather, I'm sure we would have played all day. We are both avid sports players and we would have played until blisters formed upon our hands.

Lisa, however, is getting bored sitting in her SUV. Every time Ben and I switched hitting, I would go to Lisa and tell her that it wouldn't be too much longer, although I had no idea what time we would end.

We start to gather the equipment together and I can hear Lisa shouting.

"Finally, it's time to grab some dinner. We'll order subs. Do you want to eat there or take it home?"

"We can eat it there." I add.

We drive down to Cambridge House of Pizza, a few blocks from the field. After ordering our subs, we sit down at the table and start to talk about Babe Ruth.

"Frank, do you have any idea what team might draft me?"

Lisa also has an interest in this conversation.

"What team do you think Ben will go to?"

"After talking to some of the Babe Ruth coaches, I believe Ben will be going in the first round. If I had to pick a team, I would say the Orioles. It's hard to say at this point, but due to the interest of the teams and where they lie in the draft, I'm picking the Orioles. That could change and you might be picked sooner."

"What pick do the Orioles have?"

"They currently have the fifth pick."

"I could be the fifth kid picked?"

"You could be, but I'm not sure."

"So, four players are better than me?" Ben adds with a frown.

"I never said four players are better than you. From what I've seen and heard, it just means other coaches are looking at something different. It's not who's the best player; it's who they think will be best for their team. You are definitely one of the top five kids in the league. It's just like me deciding between Juan and Eddie. It comes down to who they think will be best suited for their team. After all the times you've fought hard to be a great ball player and were picked last in the minors, and near the end in the majors, you have an opportunity to be at the top of the list. You could be top five out of fifty kids. That identifies someone who has a lot of heart and never gives up."

"Yeah, I guess so."

I change the subject.

"Any plans for the weekend?"

"Well, Ben usually goes with his grandfather on the weekends."

"*The Dark Knight* just came out a few weeks ago. I was wondering if you and Ben would like to go see the movie."

"I'm not much of a movie fan."

"Can I still go?" asks Ben, jumping in excitement.

"Lisa, would you mind if I took him to see the movie on Sunday at the IMAX theatre?"

She looks at me as if I put her on the spot; that was not my intention.

"Ben is supposed to go with his grandfather this--"

Ben abruptly interrupts her. "I'll stay if I can go to the movies with Frankie."

Lisa's facial expression says it all. "You never want to stay home with me; you always want to go over your grandfather's."

"It's because we don't do anything. I go there because I have my cousins, basketball, and the beach."

Lisa is not too happy with his reply, but her expression shows it was the truth. She looks at me, aggravated that I put her in this situation, she eventually says yes.

"Since we are talking about movies, would you like to rent a couple of movies and visit Jack at work?"

"Sure, as long as it is ok with you Ma," Ben adds.

"Yes that's fine with me."

The three of us walk into Jack's store.

As we are looking for movies, Jack asks Ben, "What are you doing this weekend?"

"We're going to see *The Dark Knight* at the IMAX theatre. Do you want to come with us?"

Jack hesitates. "I don't want to interfere."

"Frankie, can he come?" Ben asks.

"Jack, it's just going to be the three of us, Lisa doesn't want to go to the movies. You are more than welcome to join us."

Still hesitant, Jack looks over towards me and gives a nod of his head indicating that he'll go. At this point, it seems that Jack doesn't want to let Ben down.

"Alright, I'll go." He says.

Since Ben is an avid baseball player, I think he will enjoy *Field of Dreams*. Ben wants to rent *21*. At that point Jack comes over to me and whispers in my ear.

"You do know that movie has a sex scene in it, right?"

"No, I didn't know. C'mon Jack you know I don't watch movies, how else would I know?"

"I just want to make sure that you are aware of it."

"Ok, I'll tell Lisa and see what she says."

I walk over to Lisa to let her know about the movie and see what she has to say.

"Lisa, Jack is telling me that the movie Ben is picking has a sex scene, I don't know how graphic it may be but I wanted to let you know."

"How bad is it Jack?" She asks.

"It just shows body contact, nothing too extreme."

"Yeah that's fine."

Since Ben picks *21* and I pick *Field of Dreams*, I ask Lisa to pick a movie.

"No thanks. You and Ben can pick another movie."

After browsing for another ten minutes, Ben and I decide to rent *Be Kind and Rewind*. It seems like a very comical movie, Jack Black is hilarious.

We arrive back to the house and decide to watch *Field of Dreams* first. A half hour into the movie Lisa is getting bored and I can tell Ben isn't enjoying it either. I guess it's too old for his standards.

I turn over to Lisa and I whisper. "I'm going to change the movie. I can tell Ben doesn't enjoy this one."

"Ok, I'll go make some popcorn while you do that."

"That sounds like a great idea!"

"Ben, I know you do not like the movie now, but you will change your mind when you get older. Let's watch *21*. Since you picked it, I know you really want to watch it."

As we are watching the movie, the sex scene comes on and Lisa turns to me and hisses, "You didn't say it had this much nudity."

"I didn't know. Jack was the one that told you it wasn't too much for a twelve-year-old."

After we watch the movie, it is time for me to head home. During the summer, I work full time at the O' Brien school and I have to be in at eight o'clock in the morning.

"I have to head home, I'll talk to you later Lisa." I give her a kiss.

"Ben, I'll see you Sunday morning."

"I'll be ready bright and early!" He exclaims.

CHAPTER SEVENTEEN

The next day, my mother is standing on the porch on the second floor smoking a cigarette. I want to tell her about Lisa.

"Hey Ma, I have something to tell you."

"What is it?"

"I've been dating this woman for three weeks now. She is a little older than me. She has a twelve-year old son. Her name is Lisa, and her son's name is Ben. We met while I was coaching her son, and you'll laugh when you hear how we started to get together."

"How did it happen?"

"It all came about because Lisa thought I was being cheap, because she thought I didn't want to pay 30 cents for a toll. After that it just developed into constant flirting until the summer season officially ended." I explain.

"You are the only person I know that would be laughed at because someone thought you were being cheap. If people really knew you, they would know that you aren't a cheap person. You spend money on others, but I've never seen you buy anything for yourself."

"I just don't need it. I don't see the point of buying pointless items I'm not going to use."

"When are you going to invite Lisa over for dinner?"

"Honestly, I haven't thought about it. I'll bring it up the next time I talk to her. Let's plan for Saturday."

"Just let me know, I need to prepare whatever it is I'll be cooking."

"I'll let you know within the next day or so if it's going to be this weekend."

In all the years I've been dating, I have never brought anyone home to meet my mother. Most of my dates were just first dates and some of my dates were honest and said, "I'm sorry. I just don't find you that attractive."

Deep down I knew it was because I still looked like a rat. It was not as bad as when I was younger, but my bottom jaw was pushed so far back that it had created a huge overbite. I wasn't attractive. I was aware of it, but I had a great personality and someone had finally realized that.

One time I had a six month relationship with someone in 2003. No one knew about it because it was going to be long distance relationship once they graduated from Wentworth Institute of Technology. It was a mutual breakup. We understood it wasn't going to work because of the long distance. That is one of the reasons why I didn't tell anyone about it. Other than that, I never had a relationship with anyone else, that is, until now.

After talking to Lisa for twenty minutes during our usual late night chat, I decide to ask her about dinner.

"I told my mother about us, she would like you to come over for dinner."

She hesitates for ten seconds. "I really don't want to."

"Do you really not want to or are you just afraid of meeting my mother."

"It's such a huge step. I just don't know what I want to do."

"My mother is a very nice person. You have nothing to worry about. You've seen the way I treat you, I learned that from someone."

I didn't pull her arm or force her to make any decisions. I wanted her to decide on her own. I just told her what she already knew.

After talking for over an hour, Lisa finally makes her decision.

"Ok, I'll meet your mother."

"Great! Is Saturday good for you?"

"Yeah, Saturday evening works great for me."

"I'll let my mother know. Trust me you have nothing to worry about."

I tell my mother that Lisa will be coming over for dinner on Saturday.

"What should we have?" she asks.

"It doesn't matter to me."

"Ok, I'll make your favorite meal, meatloaf. At least I know you won't get sick from it."

"Real nice, Ma."

My mother's meatloaf is the best meatloaf I have ever had. This is not a biased opinion. I have had plenty of others. On three separate occasions I had meatloaf in restaurants. Two times I threw the meatloaf up. It was on the third time that it became the final straw.

The last time I had meatloaf outside of my mother's homemade meatloaf, it was in a restaurant. I came down with food poisoning because of it. Ironically, it had been on the first date I went on from the six-month relationship I had back in 2003. I never had meatloaf in a restaurant ever again.

I pick Lisa up to head over to my house for dinner. She says, "Do we really have to do this today?"

"Everything will be ok. You'll be fine. You have nothing to worry about."

As we are driving, she is holding my right hand and shaking her legs in nervous anticipation. I can feel how tense she is as we near our destination; her grip keeps getting tighter each time I speak, "We're almost there. Two more blocks."

As I pull in the driveway, she asks, "Is it too late to turn back?"

I turn to her, smile, and give her a kiss to ease her mind.

"Yes, it's too late."

I take her hand, walking towards the steps, insisting that everything will be all right. I open the door for her and I walk in front of her so I can direct her where to go. I open the back door. We walk in and my mother is waiting right in front of the door.

My mother says, "Oh wait one second!"

She goes into her room, when she comes out she takes Lisa's hand and opens it. My mother drops a quarter and a nickel into her palm. This is the perfect icebreaker Lisa needs.

She bursts into laughter and any stress she had in meeting my mother washes away. From there on out, they hit it off. They talk about Ben, baseball, and of course, me.

An hour into dinner my mother says, "I'm sorry but I have to have a cigarette." Lisa looks over towards me.

"Yes Lisa, go ahead and have a cigarette."

"You smoke?" My mother is in shock.

"Yes I do, is that a problem?"

"No, no, it's not a problem with me. It's just that Frankie can't stand cigarettes. I'm surprised he's dating someone who smokes."

"There's a funny story to that! We were at the championship game and before the game started, Frank said out of the blue, 'Who is smoking? I can smell the smoke a mile away. Someone is definitely smoking.' I said to him 'do you not like cigarette smoke?'

'I can't stand it. It is a complete turnoff to me.'

We had already made plans to go out before that incident. I didn't want to say anything since I knew he didn't like cigarettes. It wasn't until last week that I told him I smoke and that it was me that day he complained about it."

"That's true Ma. I had no idea it was her and I was complaining about it. As you know, I can't stand it. She hid it well for two weeks. Somehow she disguises the smell when I'm around her and as long as I don't smell it, I'm ok with it."

After a few hours, it is time to take Lisa home.

"Thank you for dinner, it was very good."

"You're welcome Lisa. Come back anytime and maybe you can bring Ben along."

"Yes, I will."

Lisa has to head back home because Ben will be coming back from his grandfather's tonight. Jack and I will be taking him to see *The Dark Knight* tomorrow morning.

As we head back to my car, she says, "Your mother is very nice, I was nervous for nothing."

"I tried telling you that, but you wouldn't believe me."

I pull up at her house. I open the car door and walk her back to her front door.

"I had a great time, thank you for everything."

"You're welcome Lisa. I told you that you can trust me with anything. Have a great night and I'll see you tomorrow morning when I pick up Ben."

I kiss her goodnight. I get back into my car I feel relieved that the night is over and that it was a success. At first I wasn't sure how my mother and Lisa would act towards one another. I did not know what to expect because it was the first time I had ever introduced my mother to a girlfriend.

CHAPTER EIGHTEEN

Lisa calls me a week after Ben, Jack, and I see *the Dark Knight*.

"The All-Star Tournament is right around the corner. The coach of Ben's team told Ben that he is pitching the first game against East Cambridge. Ben wants me to ask you if you can help him with his pitches before the big game."

"Yes, I can work with him. We have two weeks before the tournament. I will work with him any day you need me to."

"He's really nervous about it. Any chance you get, he'll want it."

"Ok, let's plan on two days a week for the next two weeks."

I work with Ben for those two weeks and we develop a consistently accurate fastball for him. He can throw a two-seam and four-seam fastball, but his two-seam is a little off at times. His curveball is his best pitch. He also has a decent slider. His fifth pitch, the changeup, isn't working out as well as we would like at this point.

"Are you going to be at the game?" Ben asks.

"Of course I will. I wouldn't miss it for the world."

"Can you guide me through the whole game?"

"Yes Ben, I will tell you what pitch to throw if you want me to."

"That will be great if you could!"

"Sure thing Ben, I'll be there for every batter."

During the All-Star tournament, Lisa, Ben, and I watch the minor league teams play. The minors play their games before the majors. I want to see what their opinion is on both Juan and Eddie as I point them out. During the All-Star tournament, I see Eddie's mother. Eddie's mother comes up to me and gives me a big hug and a kiss on the cheek.

Lisa sees what Eddie's mother is doing.

How have you been doing? Eddie's mother asks.

I'm doing great, just scouting the kids for the draft.

We talked for a few minutes.

Jim's mother also approaches me as well. She gives me a big hug.

"Frank, we miss you in the minors. You were such a great influence on the kids, all the kids ask about you."

"How's Jim doing?"

"It's not the same without you, he's thinking of quitting baseball after this year. He's having a hard time with Melissa."

"If you don't mind, I'll talk to him and see if I can convince him to go to the majors; Jim's such a great athlete."

"I'm sure if he was on your team, he would do well."

I'll talk to him after he plays this game.

Jim's game has just ended and I have a talk with him.

"Jim, your mother tells me that you might not play baseball next year?"

"It's just not as much fun as it was when you were coaching. Melissa is always yelling at us, I just don't like it."

"Jim, being in the majors is a great thing. There is so much more action, it is a lot better up here. Do me one favor, don't quit. Come on up to the majors for just one year, and if you don't like it, I give you permission to quit."

Jim gives me the assuring look that he will give it a shot.

"Ok Coach, I will try it for one year. Can I be on your team?"

"I can't promise that you will be, but I will try to draft you on my team. I can promise that I will try."

Jim heads over to his parents.

Ben's All-Star game is starting to get under way.

As I am rooting Ben on, Mr. Loney comes over and puts a Central Division hat on my head.

He says, "If we play Ben's team tomorrow, I'm curious to know who you will be rooting for."

"Let's take it one game at a time, you'll find out tomorrow if it comes down to that."

Everyone is starting to take pictures of me being a so-called traitor especially since I have the hat on. They take a picture of me with Lisa while I'm wearing Central's hat.

Ben is on the mound and before every pitch he looks over to me asking what he should throw. I have all kinds of signs for him: high, inside, outside, low, fastball, curveball, slider etc. and he trusts me with each and every pitch.

There is one point during the game that someone decides to talk to me during Ben's performance and Lisa interrupts the conversation, "Frank, Ben is looking over towards you for advice! Pay attention to him."

Ben pitches a three-hit complete game shutout striking out twelve batters. Central wins the game 12 – 0. Ben approaches me after the game, "That was the best game I have ever pitched! Thank you so much for helping me today!"

"Anytime Ben, you pitched a great game!"

Ben, Lisa, and I are watching my division play. Two hours later, the game ends.

Mr. Loney comes to me after their game.

"We won our game too. Who are you going to root for?"

I didn't answer him; I just gave him a smirk.

Do I root for my league or do I root for Ben's team? I can already tell tomorrow is going to be hilarious.

In the end, my league won the Inter-city league All-Star Tournament. To me, it was bittersweet. It was a great game. It was a pitcher's duel which ended in a 3 – 0 victory. I stayed as neutral as I could; rooting on both teams.

Babe Ruth coaches will now be drafting for their teams shortly after this game. It gives everyone in my league a better understanding of how many picks each team needs. Our draft is a week away, I am still having trouble deciding who I want to pick.

Lisa calls me in the middle of the week.

"Frank, Ben was picked up by the Orioles. You were right, he was the fifth kid picked. Ben's coach, Johnnie, already setup a practice for this weekend."

"That's great Lisa! I knew he would be picked in the first round. He must be excited."

"Ben is excited. What's new with you?"

"Well, my draft is two days away and I am still having a hard time deciding who I want to pick for my first pick. What's your opinion on what you saw last weekend?"

"You should pick Juan."

"Just trying to get your opinion, why should I pick Juan?"

"Well, because he's a good ball player and that's who you wanted from the very beginning."

"Yes, that is true but as the season progressed I saw potential in Eddie that I didn't see right away, and this is why it's a hard decision for me. You're not jealous of Eddie's mother are you?"

"She is very friendly around you and always gives you a hug and a kiss when she sees you."

"She's not the only mother I hug, Lisa. I hug Jim's mother all the time when I see her too, but it's because I'm a great person and nothing more than that. I intend on drafting Jim as well. I don't draft for the mothers, as you may think, I draft based on what I think will be best for the team."

"Pick whoever you want, I told you my opinion. It's your team, you decide who you want to pick," Lisa says in a jealous tone.

"I value your opinion, but understand that if I pick Eddie it's because I think he will be a better player than Juan in his final year."

"I have to go, have fun at the draft and let me know how it goes."

She hangs up without letting me say another word. She has a drastic attitude change in a matter of seconds.

With the draft in less than 24 hours, I still can't decide. It's going to be a "game-time" decision. My first pick is the hardest one to make, and as long as everything else goes according to plan, both Jim and Andre will be on the team as well. I'm prepared even if I can't draft Andre or Jim. In these drafts, everyone has to prepare for the unexpected.

CHAPTER NINETEEN

All the coaches gather in the function hall that is reserved for the draft, some of us are grab a beer and then head downstairs for the meeting. There needs to be one coach here to represent each team in order for the meeting to start. Most of the coaches anticipate my first pick to be Juan. Since the beginning of the year, Juan has been on the top of my list.

Everyone knows that I've been praising Juan's abilities for the past six months. Even Nathan, who has the pick right after me, is pretty confident that's who I'm going with. However, the past two months, Eddie has impressed me with his baseball knowledge. Clearly Juan looks like a stronger player, but Eddie is more fundamentally sound in all aspects of the game. At this very moment, within minutes before the draft is set to begin, I have yet to decide who I want to pick.

Jack asks me who we are picking; I tell him that I don't know. It's between Eddie and Juan. It's a tough pick this year. It depends on the Cardinals and who they pick first. If they stay with their pick, which I can almost guarantee, then I'm deciding between Eddie and Juan. I anticipate the Cardinals drafting a kid whose parents will be joining the coaching staff. Since Rodney has coached this player in the minors, I'm sure he will be picking him for his team in the Majors. If the Cardinals pick Eddie or Juan though, it makes my pick easier.

Damien is trying to get everyone's attention. Nathan brings in a chair for him to sit on. It is a medieval chair with red velvet upholstered fabric and gold buttons inlayed into the wood.

As Damien sits down, he tries to gather everybody's attention so the meeting can start. All of the coaches are talking amongst themselves discussing their teams' picks. Damien starts to cry; tears are streaming down his face because he's overwhelmed that no one is listening to him. His sensitive demeanor does not make him fit to be president for this league.

Nathan stands up, raises his voice and brings our attention to Damien, to start the meeting. You can always rely on the person pulling the strings to take over when need be.

The Cardinals have the first pick.

Rodney elects the player we expected, Harry. Now it's my turn to pick and without much hesitation, I quickly name Eddie as the second pick of the draft for the Giants.

I decide against my initial thoughts from months ago and what Lisa wants me to do. Besides, we've only been dating for two months now and she doesn't see the potential the players have for the Giants. It all boils down to who I think will be the better player in three years, and I believe Eddie beats out Juan.

128

After my pick, Nathan is in complete disbelief. He anticipated my pick to be Juan. He did not plan for this to happen.

Nathan in an uproar calls "TIME" then convenes with his assistant coach, Mr. Loney.

It takes ten minutes, which is the most time it has ever taken any coach in the five years I've been here to pick a player. My decision has certainly created a problem for Nathan.

With the third pick in the draft, the Astros pick Bobby; a tall player with some power. Everyone else projected him to go late in the second round; they didn't expect him to go as early as this.

Mr. Baseball then follows with the fourth pick, excited that Juan is still available in the draft; he drafts him for his team.

After two hours, the draft is over. I am able to select the other two players I want for my team: Andre and Jim. I'm confident in the players I have drafted for the Giants.

Shortly after the meeting, Nathan comes over to me and asks, "Were you just blowing smoke up my ass about Juan?"

"No sir, he's a great ball player. For a while I thought I was going to pick Juan just like everyone assumed, but these past few weeks I noticed more out of Eddie than Juan. I thought Eddie would be the better ball player in three years. From what I saw in the summer league, I noticed more out of Eddie than Juan. Why didn't you pick Juan?"

"Honestly, I never scouted him. I didn't know much about him. I assumed Eddie would be there. Knowing the fact that you were going to pick Juan, I disregarded him as an option."

I start to walk away while the other coaches come up to me and state that I threw Nathan a huge curveball. He didn't plan for that to happen. As long as the other coaches have been around, no one recalls Nathan taking so long to make a pick in the draft. I guess no one can ever expect anything going according to plan.

Just slightly after I exit the doors of the function hall, I call Lisa to let her know who I drafted. She picks up the phone and she immediately asks, "Did you pick Eddie?"

Knowing the fact that she didn't want me to, I hesitate telling her but I did.

"Lisa, I picked Eddie because I think he will be a better player than Juan in his third year in the majors. It wasn't an easy decision but that's who I went with."

"You know I didn't want you to pick him and you still did. You are also aware that I don't like Eddie's mother either but you still picked him."

She is clearly upset and without letting me try to explain why I picked Eddie, she quickly hangs up the phone in disgust. I decide not to call her back right away. I just let her be. No one is going to dictate my team because someone doesn't like the mother of the player I drafted.

We've only been dating two months and she's already getting jealous of someone else. I don't cheat on anyone, I'm completely loyal to the one person I'm with all the time. She must've had trust issues in the past. It seemed odd that she would get upset so quickly over nothing.

During one of our offseason practices, I have a conversation with Adam. Adam is in his late forties and has three children. His oldest is on my team. I drafted his son two years ago for the Giants. One thing we have in common, he's a smartass just like me. There were many times he and I would go at it, verbally making fun of one another, but in a comical manner.

"Adam, I am concerned with Lisa."

"What do you mean?"

"She told me she has a malignant brain tumor and I don't know how to react."

"Listen kid, the best advice I have is that if you feel like it's too much, you should just leave. If you just want to be with her because she doesn't have anyone else then it's the wrong reason. I know you don't know how to react, and I'm not much older than you but one thing I do know, it's not worth worrying about. She was fine before you; she'll be fine without you."

Adam is right, but I still don't know what I want to do. I like her, but I don't know if her attitude is reflective from her brain tumor. I guess I'll use the wait and see approach.

"Thanks Adam, I appreciate it."

I needed someone to give me an insight on this matter.

I don't know why I told Adam, but I felt I had to ask someone. This is a situation I've never been in before and I really don't know how to approach it.

I never told anyone else about Lisa's brain tumor. I just needed one opinion. Although Lisa told me not to tell anyone, I had to. I know Adam won't say anything. I needed to tell someone I could trust, to help guide me in the right direction to handle this accordingly.

CHAPTER TWENTY

Lisa and I have been dating for five months, and with Christmas being the first big holiday, I am not sure what to get her. I know she loves coffee. That's an easy small gift to get her, but the decision I am having trouble with is what to get her that means a lot. Our relationship has been on and off, especially when she has her bad days. I'm not sure what exactly it is, but something is definitely wrong. We never broke it off, she wanted time and like the gentleman I am, I respected her wishes. Days would pass and I wouldn't call her, but she would occasionally call me as if nothing happened.

Christmas is right around the corner and I'm sure the stress of Christmas is getting to her like it does for all families barely making ends meet to survive. If this on and off thing continues after Christmas, I will have to end it. This is not a healthy relationship to be in, and I deserve someone who wants to be with me more often than not. I don't think I did anything wrong, but she's trying to sort out whatever problems she has.

I've been working over eighty hours a week with two jobs and taking classes at Bunker Hill. I'm in over my head with my work load. I always push myself to the limit as often as I can. I'm a workhorse, and I want to make sure I can give Lisa and Ben the best Christmas possible.

As I am contemplating a big gift to get her, I turn on the TV before bed and a commercial comes on that depicts a gift that has great significance to how I feel about Lisa.

It is a diamond encrusted necklace with an open heart design and once I hear the commercial say: "If your heart is open, love will always find its way in." As corny as it sounds, it reminds me of Lisa.

I had to get it. With just a little more than a week before Christmas, I go to the nearest jewelry store to buy it.

They are all out.

Many stores are sold out because of the holiday. I drive up to New Hampshire to see if I can find one there. As I arrive at one of the stores in the mall, they are sold out, but I can order one and it will be in the store in a couple of days. Without hesitation, I say yes and I pay for it right then and there. For only a couple hundred dollars, this is the perfect gift to give her.

I feel relieved that I have found the perfect gift for her. For all the trouble I've gone through to get it, I'm going to make sure it's the last gift she opens. I will put it at the very bottom of her stocking. I can only imagine her expression when she opens it. I'm a typical last minute shopper and this is no exception.

It's Christmas Eve and I still have some shopping to do. I'm spending Christmas Eve at Lisa's house because Ben is going to his grandfather's on Christmas Day. It is one in the afternoon now and I anticipate finishing my shopping around six. I call Lisa letting her know that I'll be over at seven; I have some last minute Christmas shopping to do.

After I hang up, Lisa calls right back to say that Ben wants to talk to me.

"Can I go Christmas shopping with you?" He asks.

"As long as it's fine with your mother, you can come along."

"She already said it's ok, what time are you coming to pick me up?"

"I'm on my way. I'll be there in thirty minutes."

I pick up Ben and we head over to the Cambridge Side Galleria. I still have to get some gifts for my family and something small for Ben and Lisa. Ben already knows about the necklace I am getting for his mother. I bring the gift with me so I can show him what it looks like.

I ask him, "What do you think?"

"She'll love it. What did you get me?"

"Nice try Ben, it's not going to work on me."

"I thought I'd give it a shot."

"Who are you shopping for?"

"I still have to get something for my grandfather and some stuff for my mother and you."

As we arrive at the mall, we separate; he doesn't want me to know what store he is getting my gifts in. He has his phone, so
134

if he needs me, he can call me. We arrange to meet at the food court for lunch in an hour.

I pick up a box of baseball cards and some sports memorabilia that I know he will enjoy. I buy him a video game for his Xbox 360; he will be getting that for Christmas from his mother. I tend to spoil anybody I can during the holidays. I love giving gifts. I could care less if I receive any. The look on someone's face when I surprise them with unexpected gifts is the best gift I can get. I enjoy seeing people happy and I do whatever I can to make anyone happy, even during the darkest of times.

I make sure I pay for the gift-wrapping at the mall, especially since Ben is with me. He won't know what stores I went into. The element of surprise awaits him on Christmas Day.

We meet at the food court for lunch; he shows me what he bought for his mother and his grandfather. He bought a watch for his grandfather. He remembers how his grandfather always asks him for the time and that if he had a watch, he wouldn't keep asking him for it. It's a sensible gift to give to his grandfather. Ben then shows me a Jason Varitek shirt that he bought for his mother. Jason Varitek is her favorite Boston Red Sox player.

"I'm sure she'll enjoy that Ben."

I have to go back to my house and wrap all the gifts I have for Lisa and Ben, especially the necklace. I'm leaving this gift at my house. After we open gifts at her house, I want to make sure she has something to open when she comes over for Christmas dinner at my house.

I call Lisa to let her know our progress and that we should be home at seven as I told her earlier.

"Frank, it's been a tradition that we open all the gifts on Christmas Eve. When Ben's grandfather picks him up, he doesn't have enough time to play with some of his gifts so we make sure we open the gifts on Christmas Eve."

"I don't want to break tradition, that's fine with me.

We arrive back at Lisa's at seven.

Lisa, I have most of your gifts here but I still left some behind at my house so you will have something to open when we go there tomorrow."

As we are opening our gifts, Ben receives the Xbox 360 plus a handful of games; mostly sports games and Call of Duty. Lisa bought Ben the holiday Hess truck, which has been a tradition for her to get him every Christmas.

It seems she spent a lot of money on him alone. When I open up my gifts, there are sport pictures, Red Sox shirts and a hat, plus other gifts as well. I love all the gifts I received and I'm glad I told them if it's anything sports, I'll enjoy it.

I'm ecstatic that I didn't have to elaborate when I said anything sports. One Christmas, my family bought me a sports bra as a gag gift, boy did I ever regret not being specific that year.

Ben enjoyed his gifts. He hooked up his Xbox 360 right away.

"Do you want to play me in Madden?"

"Yeah, put it in and I'll play a game with you."

Shortly after playing the game with Ben, it's time for all of us to head to bed. It's slightly past midnight and we all have a busy morning ahead of us.

I am quite shocked with the amount of money Lisa spent on the both of us. She doesn't collect child support. She's not on any government assistance. All she has is section-8 for housing. She doesn't have a job, and most of the time she's barely putting food on the table. It's shocking to see how much she was able to spend on us. It's none of my business, but I thought it was odd. She's happy and we are happy. That's all that matters.

It's Christmas Day and Ben is being picked up at ten. After he leaves, Lisa starts to get ready. It's taking over an hour for her to get ready. Fortunately, I told my mother we would be there at 2:30. I told Lisa that dinner was at 1:30 because I knew we would be running late; I was prepared this time.

I made sure that there would be about an hour before dinner to unwrap gifts. I like to plan things ahead as best as I can. We arrive at my house close to 1:45. With a few gifts that we have to open, we finally reach the stockings, which I knew would be last.

I bombarded the top of the stocking with chocolates and gift cards so she would have a hard time getting to it. If it was hard for me to find the necklace, it will be hard for her to retrieve it.

"Is this it?" She asks not sure if there is more.

"You have to dig at the very bottom of the stocking, there's more than just chocolate there."

She puts her hand all the way to the foot of the stocking. She grabs a box wrapped in red wrapping paper with a white bow on it. She sticks a little bit of her tongue out of her mouth in anticipation of what it might be. As she tears the wrapping paper off, she sees a velvet-fur coated box.

She slowly opens the box.

Her blue eyes sparkle with amazement.

She puts her left hand over her mouth in disbelief. She can barely speak, the look is priceless.

"I...I can't believe it, it's perfect."

"I knew you would like it. I always save the best for last."

She starts to shed a tear, "This is beautiful. I can't believe anyone would treat me this well." She puts it on her neck right away and gives me a hug and a kiss.

"This is the best Christmas I've ever had."

That's all I needed to hear. I love it when people say it's the best Christmas they have ever had. That brought a big smile across my face. That was the best gift I received.

Christmas is a success.

It had to be all the stress she was dealing with prior to Christmas that made our relationship feel on and off. With my seasonal job over with, I can focus more on school work and my other job.

CHAPTER TWENTY-ONE

It's early February and it's an unusually warm day for this time of the month. It was just yesterday that we received one of the biggest snow storms of the year. As I am getting ready to go to Bunker Hill for class, I receive a phone call from Lisa. She's in a frantic state of mind.

"Somebody hit my car during the snowstorm last night."

"Are you ok?"

"I'm fine. Both Ben and I were sleeping when it happened. When I was getting ready to drive Ben to school in the morning he noticed that the car door was smashed in."

She is crying hysterically.

"I don't have the money to fix my car. I don't know how I'm going to afford the deductible."

All of a sudden she directs the conversation towards our relationship.

"I don't want to talk to you anymore. I have to figure out what to do."

Instead of going to class, I decide to visit her and make sure she is calmer. Once I arrived, I notice her SUV parked on the side street. I can barely get close enough to her car door, there was already a foot of snow on the ground before last night's storm. We are having one of the worst February snow totals in recent years.

I notice yellow marks on the passenger side door. There are two significant indentations created from the impact on the door. I take a few pictures with my phone. I want to try and investigate it when I have time. After I finish observing Lisa's SUV, I head towards her apartment. As I am walking to her porch, I notice that she is already talking to a police officer.

As I approach her, I give her a kiss on the cheek and a rose that I had picked up from the nearest flower shop.

"Are you ok?" I ask her again.

"I'm feeling better now. I'm still upset that my car, my baby, is damaged."

The police officer is asking a series of questions.

"Do you know when this happened?"

"It happened sometime last night when my son and I were sleeping."

"Do you know anybody who would've done this?"

It takes Lisa a while to answer that question.

"I think it was a bus that did it." She finally says.

From what I notice as she gives her answer, it is obvious to me that she knows who would do something like this but she doesn't want to say it.

"The markings on the SUV are yellow. It had to be a bus."

To me, she is disregarding the question at hand and directing the attention towards what she wants the officer to think it could be. I find her answer very peculiar.

The police officer responds. "I will have someone call the MBTA and ask for an investigation to be conducted into the matter to determine if it was a driver that did this."

A few days pass. While I am examining the pictures of Lisa's car, I am confident that it wasn't a bus that did the damage. The indentation is too irregular to come from a bus. From Lisa's action and tone of voice in answering the officer, she knows that somebody did this on purpose, but why?

Mysteries are exciting to me. I like to try and figure things out. If it wasn't a bus and Lisa alluded that she knew who might have hit her car on purpose, then something is not right.

After having a conversation with Ben, he confides in me that he knows who could have done it. After many years of dealing with the hostility of his mother's ex-boyfriend, Ashley, Ben has a feeling that it could be him. He tells me it's because Ashley has been calling his mother lately.

"He was with my mother just a week before she started dating you; I think they're talking again. I can't stand him and I wish that my mother would stop talking to him. He always hands me hundred dollar bills when he comes over." Ben explains.

He is very descriptive of the physical abuse he witnessed when his mother and Ashley were together in the past. He recalls a situation when Ashley was over one night extremely drunk; he yelled at Lisa at the top of his lungs, flung her on the bed and forced her down with all his weight, saying that she should always listen to him or else. Ben ran into the other room, grabbed his wooden bat and went to defend his mother. Before he had the chance to swing the bat at Ashley, Lisa insisted to Ben to drop the bat, and then yelled at Ashley to leave them alone.

After hearing this conversation from Ben, I look up his name. To my surprise, Ashley Mela is retired. He had worked for the City of Cambridge. His father also resided in the city with a position of power but passed away suddenly a few years ago. I also discover that Ashley purchased a permit to use a plow attachment on his truck during snow storms. Interestingly enough, a plow fits the dimensions of the damage on Lisa's SUV.

With that information, I am more than certain it was Ashley who hit Lisa's truck.

Just a week after the incident, I receive a text message from Lisa saying that we shouldn't date anymore:

It's not you, it's the situation I'm in. I can't get out of it.

Before I can respond, Lisa calls me within seconds of sending her text. She says, "No matter what I do, I can't get out of it. I'm stuck and have no other choice."

With Ashley's connections to the city, he knows he won't get into trouble for what he did. He stresses to her that no matter what she tries to do, she will always regret any action that she brings upon him.

There is nothing I can do, so I let it be. Even before Christmas I know more problems can arise and if so, I am going to back away.

I do just that.

I don't know the extent of the situation or what she has gotten herself into. The best solution would be to back away. As of late February 2009, we officially ended our seven month relationship.

It's obvious now that Lisa was paid monies to be with Ashley. Ashley is thirty years older than her. It seems that Ashley, for the lack of a better term, is her pimp. Now it makes sense why Lisa was able to spend that much money during Christmas. With Ashley's ties to the city and the legal document which is needed for anyone to have a snow plow in the city, he feels like he has all the power and abuses it constantly. It's time someone stops sweeping it under the rug.

It's been two months since we broke off our relationship. I knew it was over and I wasn't trying to save anything. I had moved on with my life and I would never want to get back with Lisa.

After being with her for seven months, I realize that she's a woman who listens to her rice krispies. I'm glad I got out of the relationship when I did. I can only imagine what would have happened if it went on any longer.

Ashley was involved with the crazy problems that had been happening to Lisa and there is nothing I can do, nor is there anything I want to do. It's none of my business now. If Lisa doesn't want to report it to the police, there's a reason. It is best I just leave the situation alone.

Lisa calls me on rare occasions and asks me how everything is going. She tells me that Ashley doesn't know we are talking to one another because being with Ashley is not a choice.

Lisa confides in me that Ashley is divorced and that she talks to his ex-wife about how abusive he is to women. Ashley's ex-wife left him because she couldn't stand the abuse. Lisa also tells me that he is impotent. It is information I don't need to know and I don't know why she's telling me this.

I never call her, she always calls me. When a relationship is over, I do not pursue it any further. Especially with what I've been through, it's definitely not worth anymore of my time.

CHAPTER TWENTY-TWO

It's Mother's Day 2009 and I am awoken by a phone call from Lisa.

"Why did you call Ashley and leave him a voicemail on his phone?"

"What are you talking about? I didn't leave any voicemail on anybody's phone."

I don't even like to leave voicemails when I call the parents of my team, I just call them back when I can. I adamantly deny such a thing.

"Ashley was over my house last night and when he went home he realized there was a voicemail. At that point he called me and said, 'Your fucking ex-boyfriend just left a voicemail on my phone.' That is why I am calling you. He's coming back over here with the voicemail to confirm if it was you or not. I'll call you back."

"Well, you'll hear that it wasn't me and I have no idea who would even leave him a voicemail. I don't even have his number."

Lisa calls me back thirty minutes later. "I confirmed to Ashley that it was not you who left that message. I--"

Ashley takes the phone away from her mid-sentence and says, "I was getting my balls sucked when you left that message."

"It wasn't me man. I don't know what you are talking about."

"Next time you threaten me, it will be the last time you do it."

Lisa gets back on the phone. "Do you know who would've left him a message?"

"No, I have no idea. What did it say?"

"It said that if you don't leave me or my son alone, you're dead."

"I wouldn't threaten anyone. I have no idea who would."

The phone quickly hangs up on her end.

Many friends and coaches know his name, but I never had his number, nor would I have a reason to get it. Somebody did this without my knowledge, and I would never be a part of such a thing.

I tell my friends that Lisa and I are not in a relationship anymore. We are done. My friends know that. I want someone who will love me for more than half the time. She clearly does not have the mental stability to love just one person.

146

Jack calls me a few days later. "Why would you get my cousin involved with your problems?"

"What are you talking about? You know I don't get anyone involved with my life. I never have. I never will."

"My cousin has to go to court because of you."

"STOP IT JACK! Do you even know what you are saying right now? Does it make any sense for me to do such a thing like that? If you have the audacity to blame me for something, make sure you know the god damn truth."

I never put anyone up to anything. We've been friends for twenty years and he's blaming me for his cousin's actions. This is absurd.

Jack's cousin has a history of anger issues; he's only sixteen. I have no idea why Jack's cousin would get involved; it's none of his business.

Shortly after I found out Jack's cousin had to go to court for his wrongdoings, I was getting phone calls from a Cambridge number for weeks on end. After having enough of these prank phone calls and even though no one ever left a voicemail, I changed my number.

I forgot to delete Lisa's number after I changed it. When I sent a mass text to everyone to make them aware of the new number, I sent one to her as well. She would call me from time to time, but I never had any other problems with phone calls from Cambridge. I knew it was Ashley behind them.

After months of trying to find a connection with me, Ashley later gave up trying to involve me with something I had nothing to do with.

Even though I had no connection to that voicemail, I am still being blamed for it. If anyone knows me, and knows me well, I do everything independently. I never ask for any assistance, it's just who I am.

I receive a phone call.

It's Ben. I haven't talked to him in three months and he must've gotten my number from Lisa's phone.

"Hey Frankie, my mom is talking to Ashley now and he's demanding her to show him where you live."

"She is Ben?"

"Yes, she's telling him what kind of car you drive and she said that she doesn't want him to damage your vehicle like he did to her truck. She also said that she would show him where you live but if she does that, she wants nothing to do with him anymore."

"Ben, I don't have my car anymore, it died a couple of weeks ago. I moved in with my aunt a couple of months ago because of the financial situation I was in, plus she lives twenty five miles away from you."

If Ashley is upset now, I can only imagine the look on his face after he finds out I don't live there anymore.

Ben is ecstatic and says softly, "That's great! I don't want him to hurt you like he's hurt us."

As sad as that sounds, he is just looking out for me. I only know one story that Ben has told me, I can only imagine what else Ashley has done to him and Lisa.

"Thank you Ben and I appreciate all that you've done for me. If anything else is going to happen that you think I should be

148

aware of, please let me know. I can't thank you enough for all you have done, do well in school and don't get into any trouble."

He hangs up suddenly, which I expected would happen. Ashley is the person behind all of this. I can't imagine a man would stoop so low to control a woman. This should not happen, no matter the situation. This man deserves to be punished. Since he didn't do anything to me, I can't do anything. Lisa knows she can go to the police. I feel that she doesn't go to the police because if Ashley has ties to the city, there's no way out for her. She's stuck in a bind and no one can help her. It's a sad world we live in when a man can control a woman to the point of slavery.

Ashley became so irate that he couldn't tie me to the voicemail that was left on his phone; that he was trying to take matters into his own hands.

The evidence is overwhelming. I can easily take Ashley to court and have Lisa's son as a witness of Ashley's actions. But I would not put a thirteen year-old child in a court room just to prove how much of a nuisance Ashley is to everyone. That could cause a traumatic problem for Ben. It's not my place to do anything.

A few weeks later Lisa calls me.

"Frank, how have you been?"

"I'm ok, hanging in there."

"Did you move?"

"Yes I did."

"Where did you move to?"

"I'm not going to tell you. I have no reason to tell you."

The conversation only lasts a few minutes, if that. I know why she called. Ashley must've told her to call me and find out where I live. Ben knows I moved, but he doesn't know where. I wasn't going to fall for her trap. I knew better.

CHAPTER TWENTY-THREE

This season Jack has parted ways with the Giants. He has an opportunity to take over the Nationals after Jerry retires at the end of the season. Jerry has been a coach in the league for many years, but the thing that bothered me about his style of coaching was that he always yelled at the kids when they made a mistake. That is not the way to coach. Not in my opinion. His aggressive style is the worst in the Majors that I have seen in the two years I've been managing the Giants.

People have their own way of coaching and I completely understand that. But the one thing that really bothers me, more than anything, is that every time a player, on his team or not, makes a play, even if it's striking out, Jerry hits the player on the ass. That should not be allowed. These are ten to twelve year old kids and Jerry hits them on the ass after every single play. That bothers me.

The only thing I would do, if anything at all, is either high-five or fist-pump a player who did a good job. That's the closest I would ever come to congratulating a player on a great play. For years Jerry has been doing this, and it really bothers me. I can only imagine how it bothers the parents. If I had a son, I would never want any coach to hit him on the ass. There's no reason for that. It doesn't make any sense at that age or any age for that matter.

I'm happy for Jack to have an opportunity to take over a team. I can just envision the epic battles that we will compete in, mostly for bragging rights when we play one another four times a year, excluding the playoffs.

This season starts off with one of our pitchers, twelve-year-old Carlos, struggling quite a bit. After his second game pitching, we take him off the pitching staff to work with him further, to try and develop his skills in a timely manner. The coaching staff knows Carlos can be a great pitcher.

After working with him for nearly four weeks, we thought it would be best for him to go against the worst team in the league. Hopefully playing the Pirates and doing well will boost his confidence.

Carlos shuts down everybody; his delivery is a lot better. He follows through without a problem, and his speed has increased dramatically. Carlos looks like the pitcher we all thought he would be. Even though it's his first game back in four weeks, this is a great sign.

Carlos seems like he is getting better each and every game he pitches. There's been an overwhelming debate on who is the best pitcher in the league; both pitchers are on the Giants. I wish we had this problem in the beginning of the season, but with Carlos struggling, I didn't want to jeopardize his confidence too soon. I believe I chose the right time to bring him back into the rotation. It seems that I made the right decision.

We, the Giants, are having a great year. This is the first season that we are finishing with a winning record. At this point, we are 10 – 5 with one more game to go. The last game of the season and we are playing Jack's new team, the Nationals, also with a 10 – 5 record, for the golden ticket to the Mayor's Cup tournament.

Carlos can't pitch this game since he pitched the last game. Our second ace, as some would say, is pitching in one of the most important games this season.

Jesse has been our ace all year. He's carried our team for most of this season. Without him, we wouldn't be in this position to go to the Mayor's Cup tournament. It's a great thing for him to end the regular season pitching one of, if not the biggest, games of the year.

We ultimately lose 4 – 3 in the bottom of the 6th inning on a sacrifice fly. I think I could've coached the game a little better, but I don't dwell on what would have or could have happened. What's done is done. Now we have to get ready for the playoffs. We are the number one ranked team in the playoffs.

I have a lot on my mind.

Jack and I haven't talked much since he thought I put his cousin up to calling Ashley. Jack is my best friend, if anything he should have known better. All the years he's known me, he knows that I would never tell anybody to do something for me.

His cousin is only sixteen, and at that age, teenagers blame everyone except themselves for their mistakes. Jack will come to terms with it sooner or later.

At the beginning of the year the league asked Jack and I if we would like to be the summer league coordinators, we agreed.

We would soon start going over the teams and begin gathering coaches for them. Since the league had their own agenda last year, I wanted to make sure the teams were constructed fairly this year and years to come. With that in mind, that is why Jack and I elected to be summer league coordinators and because of that, we are now on the Board of Directors.

Right before we start the playoffs, Adam comes up to me.

"Hey Frank, I have a situation that has come up and I was wondering if you could babysit my three kids next week. My wife's work screwed up her vacation schedule and with the kids out of school, we need someone to babysit them for six hours a day, Monday through Friday. Are you available? I will pay you, that won't be a problem."

Right now, I am only working part-time at the school in the afternoon and I could use some extra cash. Full-time at the school doesn't start until the second week of July.

"Yes Adam, I can babysit your children. That's not a problem."

"Thanks Frank, I appreciate it."

With working at the O'Brien school in just the afternoon, it gives me plenty of time to babysit his kids and go to work right after.

We flew through the playoffs. We won three games in a row. We had the best pitching staff going into the playoffs and we shut down nearly every team. I can honestly say if Carlos was pitching all year the way he has been for the second half of the season, we would have easily gone to the Mayor's Cup. But I will always sacrifice a Mayor's Cup to make sure a player's confidence is at their peak each and every year. It's more important to me for a kid to build confidence in himself than putting him back in the game too soon and possibly ruin his confidence for years to come. I made the right decision to wait as long as I did. We went undefeated in the playoffs and captured our first championship trophy since I took over as manager.

I dealt with a lot this year with Lisa and Ashley, and even Jack blaming me for something I had nothing to do with.

It was really devastating to me that my best friend would accuse me of putting anyone up to something like that. I've always been independent with my actions. I will never change that about myself.

Baseball helped me get through this ordeal. I focused more on baseball than I did anything else. I suppose when bad things happen in your life, your attention can be directed somewhere else. I'm glad to say, baseball was my savior this year.

CHAPTER TWENTY-FOUR

Two months pass and nothing else has happened since Ben called me in May. The players I drafted: Eddie, Andre, and Jim, were a major factor in the Giants winning the playoffs for the first time since I took over as the manager.

After coaching the A team for the second straight year, Jerry, the manager of the Mayor's cup qualifying team, asks me to join his staff to coach the All-Star game since I know the players who will be playing the game in September. I accept the offer to be an assistant coach for the All-Star team.

The Inter-City All-Star game is played in the middle of September. This year the tournament is being held on the field I coach during the regular season.

It is a warm and sunny Saturday afternoon and there are crowds of people gathering to watch the four games that will take place throughout the day.

About an hour before the 3rd game is about to start, I see Lisa coming towards me. She's with her new boyfriend, Johnnie, Ben's new coach.

As I am watching the game, Lisa separates from Johnnie behind home plate and comes closer to me.

"Can I talk to you?"

I think to myself, what could go wrong? In front of a crowd of people that know me, I'm curious to know what Lisa has to say.

Hesitantly I say, "Sure."

Larry, who is a friend of mine, is ten feet away watching Lisa while our conversation is taking place. I didn't ask him to be there, but he knows this doesn't look good.

We walk into the parking lot. She wants to get away from everyone else.

She states, "Why can't you stop trying to contact me? Why can't you and your friends leave me alone?"

"Lisa, you know that's not true. I don't even know why you're bothering me with this."

I act as nonchalant as I can be, in a calm demeanor shaking off anything and everything she has to say. I know Ashley put her up to this. If he didn't, she's crazier than I thought.

It takes a lot for me to get upset at anything. I never get into an argument with anyone. I'm always calm while being verbally attacked because it's not going to make the situation any better. If I escalate my voice, it will only make things worse, plus that's what the other person wants, and I never give anyone the satisfaction of yelling back. Once someone tells me something that's not true, my sarcasm and smart ass remarks peak at its best.

"I have no idea what you are talking about, and when you said you were in a bind that you couldn't get out of, I didn't want to be a part of that relationship anymore. It was over and I took it as that. I don't continually pursue someone who doesn't want anything to do with me. This was over months ago. I could care less about you. Let me ask you this, if I keep contacting you, why haven't you gone to the police?"

She stutters; she doesn't know how to respond. Before she is able to reply, I continue the conversation: "You're just as crazy as people say you are and you're making it easier for everyone to believe it. Your attitude further interests my curiosity. What else do you have to say that I can laugh at you about?"

She starts pointing towards my friend Jack and says, "How come I keep getting these phone calls from your 500 pound fat friend who keeps leaving me voicemails?"

At this point deep down, I'm livid. I don't care if people make fun of me, I deal with that. But do not make fun of my friends at all. I will always be by my friends' sides especially when I know someone is lying.

I would never give anyone's phone number out without that person giving me permission. With my usual smart ass remarks I state: "He's right over here, let's go ask him! Or are you too afraid to address the situation yourself?"

She quickly blabbers something else to change the subject. I abruptly stop her godforsaken mental block.

"I have an idea, why don't you take him to court. That is of course if the phone records indicate so, but you're lying about that just like the brain tumor you said you had last year. I'm sorry Ashley has you tied down. I guess you just like being his little bitch. Only you can get yourself out of the jam you're in. You must like being slapped around like a little whore, because I know I wouldn't enjoy it if I were you. I'm not going to believe a word you have to say. You might as well stop your tirade, although I find the habitual lies you're coming up with extremely funny, it has to stop. Since I don't believe anything you say, just do something about it, you're a mature lady… oh that's right you're just a lady, what was I thinking. I am not going to give you the satisfaction of trying to bring me down in front of my friends. Jack would never leave messages on anyone's phone. You are not going to ruin any friendship of mine. So get off my field and leave me alone."

"Why did you hire a hit man to kill me?"

"I hired a hit man to kill you?! This is amazing. Your lies just keep getting better. I only have a part-time job and I have no car, but I have the money to hire a hit man? Why would I hire a hit man on you, when you are supposed to be dying anyway?"

I start walking away.

"I'm not done talking to you!"

"I have nothing else to say to you, Lisa. Just leave me alone."

She walks away in disgust. She did not anticipate my reactions to go as smoothly as they did. I got the best of her this time. She tried to have me erupt into a mad man and because I didn't, it pissed her off even more.

I told her the truth and in front of all my friends.

I head over to the field trying to gather myself from the tirade Lisa just put on. I have an All-Star game in which I am an assistant to Jerry and Jack. I have some time to figure out why Lisa would do such a thing. As I sit down, Melissa, Kim, Jack, Rodney, and Larry come over to me and ask if I'm alright.

They've never seen me this uptight before. I only get uptight when I am defending myself. It doesn't happen often, but when it does, I make sure the person on the other end is aware that they are wrong.

Although Larry was watching the conversation, he didn't hear much of what was being said. I never told Jack what Lisa said about him. I never told anyone what was said. I kept it to myself. Even though the coaches asked what was said, all I replied with was: "Lisa was trying to cause a scene and I didn't let her get to me. It's over now. It's time for me to try and focus on the game."

Jerry comes over to where I am sitting down.

"Frank, I need your opinion. Should Jesse or Carlos pitch for this game?"

"Jerry, at this point I believe it doesn't matter who we pitch. If it were me, I would go with Jesse."

"Ok Frank, I will have Jesse pitch this game."

My head is now focusing on the game at hand. But I am still bothered by Lisa and her crazy antics. There has to be a reason why she did that. I'll figure it out. There's a reason for everything. But for now, I must focus on being the bench coach for the Inter-City All-Star game that is about to start.

Jesse is having the best game of his life. He's pitching a no-hitter in the top of the 5th inning. Everything is smooth sailing. We are up 9 – 0. During the inning, Jack tells the shortstop to move over to his right. I don't know why he would tell the shortstop to move at this stage of the game, especially considering the nine run lead we have, but I'm just the bench coach. Jack is deserving of being an assistant to Jerry since this will be his team next year. That is why I don't say anything to Jack. It's his team that made the Mayor's Cup, rightfully so, he should say what he chooses as an assistant coach for the All-Star team.

Just seconds after that, the ball is hit to the left of the shortstop. The shortstop runs over to the ball but he misses it by inches as it slowly goes into left field.

Jesse's no-hitter is broken up and he is devastated. Jack is beating himself up over the decision he just made. Jesse ends up striking out ten batters and giving up the lone hit. We win the game 10 – 0. We are headed to the Inter-City All-Star Championship game tomorrow.

As the game ends, an epiphany strikes me as to why Lisa did what she did. I realize that it was all a game to her. I believe she was staging it so that I would call her for the first time in seven months. I realize that her thought process prior to the argument was to make me feel upset so that I would call her and apologize for my friend calling her and leaving her messages. But I knew it wasn't true. She wanted me to think it was.

If I were to call her, like she wanted me to, she could address it to the police that I'm harassing her. Even though I wouldn't be harassing her, it would seem like I was since the phone records would have indicated so. That would've just been the perception, because that is what I believe Ashley told her to do.

I figured out why she would do it and it doesn't seem that farfetched. I am by no means stupid and I didn't fall for it. I continued my life without falling into any traps of hers. When she told me in the past that she had a few restraining orders out on some men, this must have been how she started them all.

CHAPTER TWENTY-FIVE

October 9, 2009, it is a chilly Friday morning and the wind is stronger than usual. I walk into the best donut shop in Cambridge, Verna's Donut Shop, which I visit frequently during the week to get my favorite and the most notoriously known glazed donut around town. As I am enjoying the glazed donut and reading the Boston Herald, I receive a phone call from my boss, Kim.

"Frank do you have any idea what's been going on since late last night?"

"No, I have no idea, what's going on?"

"I think it's best if you just come in and we talk about it then."

"Ok, I'll be there in 30 minutes."

I look at my phone for the time and it's only 9:15 in the morning. It has to be important if she wants to see me five hours before work.

I rush over to work as soon as I can. I have no idea what's going on, and if she couldn't tell me over the phone, it must be serious.

As I walk into the office in a frantic state of mind, I turn to Kim. "What's the problem?"

I am standing in front of her desk trying to catch my breath from running the ten blocks to get here. She hands me this plastic coated piece of paper which I start to read:

WANTED

"Information on this man below: He is a COACH here in Cambridge and has been accused of molesting a child. He may have other victims who have not come forward. If your child was/is in contact with this man, they may be in danger. A few other people have come forward stating this man, Frank Glover has paid their minor children to buy ILLEAGEL DRUGS, call people and threaten BOTTLEY HARM (which was taken to court already) and he is still a coach working with our children. If you have any information on this man PLEASE call the Cambridge Police at (555) 349-1212 and ask to speak to a detective. We need to keep our children SAFE!"

I am completely taken aback by this flyer. I am struck by such a distasteful act from a human being. I sit down, shocked by what I have just read.

Kim comes over and gives me a hug.

"I'm sorry. Is there anything I can do?"

I'm dazed and confused by this flyer. I don't understand why anyone would do something like this.

The flyer has two pictures of me practicing baseball with kids. These two pictures of me were copied from the Cambridge baseball website that I am affiliated with. One picture is when I was wearing the Central Division hat that Mr. Loney put on my head.

Whoever this person is, he or she doesn't know how to spell. Illegal, Grover, and bodily were spelled wrong. It is obvious to me that this flyer was created by an older person due to the fact that whenever you put a phone number on a flyer, you don't need to put a parenthesis for the area code. In this generation, people don't do that anymore. Also, there are no reports regarding such a crime that was supposedly committed. The number listed is not a detective's phone number, but the non-emergency police number.

After being in shock for what seemed like forever, Kim shakes my shoulder repeatedly.

"Frank, you should go to the school officer and file a report and hopefully something positive comes out of this."

As I am walking towards the office, I am trying to figure out who would do this and why. I can only think of two people: Lisa and/or Ashley. I know Lisa tried to have me yell back at her last month but I didn't fall for it. I just can't see her putting up this flyer. I don't think she would do that. If she did and got caught, Ben wouldn't have a parent to take care of him. It has to be Ashley. But why would he do this?

Was he upset that he was wrong when he tried to tie me to that voicemail five months ago? Jack recently told me that his

165

cousin just finished going to court because of Ashley. It's the only thing that makes sense to me. Ashley tried to connect me to the voicemail. Is he too stubborn to admit that he was wrong? Is he trying to think of a new way to ruin my life? I can picture him doing this, from what Ben has told me in the past of Ashley's aggressive behavior, I believe Ashley is capable of doing something like this.

I walk into the office, which is located in the front of the school, I hand the police officer the flyer.

"Kim says I should come to you about this."

She looks at it and then pulls out a pad of paper and starts to write.

"Who do you think is behind this flyer?"

"Ashley Mela."

"Why do you think she's behind this?"

"Actually, it's a guy."

She pauses.

"Really? It sounds like a girl's name to me."

"Yeah, maybe his parents wanted him to be a girl. Who knows."

She starts scratching something out on her note pad.

"Why would he post up these flyers?" She asks.

"Try and stay with me on this. It's a long drawn-out process, but this is the only thing that makes sense to me." I explain.

"Ashley is thirty years older than Lisa. He was jealous that she was happy with the relationship her and I had. At one point he hit her SUV with his plow, but she didn't report it, even

166

though I'm confident enough to say it was him. He hit her SUV as a warning to get out of the relationship that she was in with me. Which, at that point, our relationship was broken off and I kept it that way."

"I didn't want to deal with her anymore. A few months go by and Ashley thought I was behind a voicemail that had some sort of threatening message. Lisa calls me that morning thinking it was me, later discovering it was not me after she heard the voicemail. She told Ashley that it wasn't me who left the message."

"When Ashley couldn't connect me to the message, he became irate at the situation and tried to hit my car as he did to Lisa's. The only reason I knew Ashley was trying to damage my car was because Ben, Lisa's son, called me to warn me that he overheard his mother and Ashley talking over the phone. After Ashley tried numerous times to find my car, he had Lisa call me to ask me if I had moved, which I did, but I wouldn't tell her where I moved to. Once Ashley found out he couldn't do anything to my car, he convinced Lisa to come to the baseball field to try to trick me into calling her and apologizing for my friends harassing her, which never happened to begin with. If I did that, he could have her go to the police and say that I was harassing her and the phone records would've indicated it. That could have entailed a restraining order."

"I didn't fall for that in September. Since Ashley never got his way, this is how he's doing it. With his connections to the city, and being a former city worker, he believes he can get away with anything, and that's why I believe he's involved with putting up the flyers."

I take a deep breath.

Thirty seconds go by.

"Is that all?" She asks.

She looks at me, with her eye brows lifted upward and her eyes telling a story that this is one crazy situation, wondering if I'm done.

"Yes, that's all. Is it not enough?"

"Oh no no, that's more than I expected. It seems like it is an interesting story."

"An interesting story...I wish I had that kind of an imagination. I couldn't make up that story if I tried."

As we are finishing up the report, Maya from the office knocks on the door. She saw me coming in to talk to the police officer as I walked by her desk an hour ago.

"There's a phone call from Kim telling me to tell you that another flyer has been found..."

She's confused to what is going on; she doesn't know exactly what Kim means by this.

The police officer wraps up the report we just finished and I start heading towards Kim's office.

"Where has the flyer been found?" I ask.

"At our baseball field."

"Comeau Field?"

"Yes, Comeau field."

Comeau field is the Major league diamond, whereas the minor league diamond is Samp Field.

After hearing that, Maya comes walking into Kim's office.

"Frank, the officer told me what's going on. I'm just finishing work now, do you want me to drive you around the city to see if we can find anymore that may be posted?"

"Yes Maya, that would be great. Thank you."

As we are leaving the school, a few people have heard what is going and they offered to help any way they can.

Maya works with the school, but I know her mostly from baseball. She would always be at the field because her husband coached in the league. We don't see her too often anymore after her husband retired. She's a high-spirited individual that jumps to anyone's side whenever she can.

Maya and I leave the school, we head towards her car. We drive to Comeau field. There we look at all the telephone poles, the generator at the football field, anywhere possible where we could see the flyers from a distance. We have come across two flyers at the field. There is a flyer on a telephone pole on each base side of the diamond.

Each flyer is taped up in a plastic sleeve wrapped around the telephone pole so securely that it takes ten minutes to remove each one. I found a third flyer posted in front of the football field; there is a camera that points in the direction of the flyer.

After searching the entire area, we didn't find any more flyers in this location. We head back to Maya's car.

"Where do you want to go now?"

"Let's go to Raymond Park, if you don't mind?"

"No not at all."

Raymond Park is another baseball field that is ten blocks away. It is a park that we used to play at quite often in the past, but since our new park was reconstructed last year, we very rarely use it these days.

Maya and I are viewing the grounds of this area and we come across two flyers that are posted on each end of the entrances.

Again, the flyers are taped vigorously around the pole. Throughout the day, Maya and I spend nearly four hours going to parks, schools, local donut shops, restaurants, and bus stops.

In just four hours, I am completely exhausted from retrieving close to thirty flyers.

Maya and I finally call it a day and head back to the school. By that time, everyone knows what is going on and they are coming up to me and asking if I'm ok, and if there is anything they can do to help.

I take the rest of the day off from work. I head to the train station to go home to Rockland.

I feel like someone is watching me on the train. I have no idea where other flyers may be but I feel like some people recognize me but they don't know how. I don't say anything. I'm just trying to go home without any problems.

My mother is able to pick me up at the Braintree station. I won't tell her what happened to me today. I don't want her getting worried about something she can't control. I'm just going to be the energetic person I always am.

As my mother and I make it home, my aunt and uncle are waiting for us at the dining room table.

My aunt says, "Hey Frankie, we've been waiting for you guys to come home! It's time for you to get your ass kicked in dominoes!"

It's just something to get my mind off of what happened to me earlier in the day. I still can't believe that in one month since Lisa and her tirade tried to get the best of me, that something else has been done to me.

This is something so unbelievable that if the wrong people get the wrong information, this could ruin my reputation of being a great coach and create something so heinous and so devastating that it may create a permanent misperception to others.

During the course of the weekend, I receive close to twenty phone calls from friends throughout the city saying they found a flyer and that they tore it down from where it was posted. My friends are asking me what I want them to do with the flyer. I tell them to hold on to it, for now.

Sunday morning my phone rings again. It's Rose, one of my friends.

"Yes, Rose?"

"I'm in front of Paddy's pub and I found a flyer. Someone had to have noticed who put it up. It was placed in between the inside and outside doors. Someone had to have seen something. I'm going to go in while I'm on the phone with you."

"Ok, I'll try and listen."

"Excuse me...did anyone happen to notice who put this flyer up on the door?" Rose asks the men at the bar.

"Can I see it?"

I hear one man asking to see the flyer. He must've shown everybody that was within the vicinity of him. Everyone at the bar starts to laugh at the flyer.

My friend is quite upset at their reaction. I can hear her as she sighs.

The person at the bar says, "Whoever it may be, just have them take a spelling test and then you'll know who put up the flyer."

The crowd laughs even louder at this point.

Leave it be, nothing is gained on someone witnessing the culprit who put up the flyers.

"Sorry Frank, I thought I could help."

"It's ok Rose, I know you were just trying to help. I appreciate it."

"What do you want me to do with the flyer?"

"Hold on to it until I find out from the detective on what to do with it."

I call the detective. I leave a message since he doesn't answer, "Detective Douglas, this is Frank Grover and I'm calling in regards to the flyers that have been posted about me. I was wondering what you would like me to do with the rest of the flyers that have been found. I know you already have a few that the school officer gave to you. I was curious to know what you want me to do with the rest."

Hours later I receive a phone call.

"Can I talk to Frank Grover?"

"Speaking sir."

172

"Frank, this is Detective Douglas. You can start throwing out the flyers as you find them."

"Ok sir, is that it?"

"Once you have a second, can you e-mail the locations of where you retrieved these flyers? I would like to know so I can check any surveillance in that area."

"Yes I can do that. It's not a problem. I will do it later today."

"That'll be great. Thanks."

As I hang up the phone, I am curious to know why I should be throwing out the flyers. I think to myself, isn't that evidence?

Nevertheless, I call Rose back.

"Rose, the detective said I should throw out the flyers. You can throw them out at this point."

"Are you sure?"

"No, I'm not sure, but that's what he said."

"Ok, I will."

"Thanks Rose."

Even though the detective said to throw out the flyers, I wasn't completely convinced I should. I kept some just in case I needed them. I don't know why I kept them, but I felt like I had to.

I send the detective an email of where I found the flyers:

Detective Douglas,

Here are the places you asked me to send to you where the flyers were found: Comeau Field, Samp Field, Dunkin Donuts at Alewife Brook Parkway, Dunkin Donuts on Mass Ave in Cambridge before the Arlington Line, Verna's Donut Shop, and at the two high schools in Cambridge. I found flyers at every school all around town. Every train station and bus stops there were flyers. There was plenty of surveillance in the area as I was retrieving the flyers. There shouldn't be much of a problem seeing who posted them up.

Thanks for all your help on the matter!
Frank Grover Jr.

CHAPTER TWENTY-SIX

As I arrive for work Tuesday afternoon, I walk into Kim's office.

"Frank, can you shut the door?"

I lean over to my right and push the door shut with my right arm.

"Frank, we need to talk about what happened last week. We have to talk about how we are going forward with this. Just earlier today there were two families who both came from England this past year and are petrified for the safety of their children. I told both families what happened to you, and what's going on. This would only be the start of questions from many parents as well as any children that might have seen such a horrific poster. A twelve year-old kid came to me at the school on Thursday and started crying in front of me. That is when I first found out about the flyers. He said, 'Tell me this isn't true,

Frankie wouldn't do this right?' I told him that you wouldn't do anything like that and it's not true."

"Kim, what does this mean in regards to my job or even coaching?"

"I don't know, but I did have to call my boss and let her know what happened and what is going on. All she told me was that we have to wait and see what response we get from the police and go from there."

"With coaching, you're going to have to ask Damien. We all know it's not true, but we have to look into the matter regardless to check the basis of such accusations."

"Do what you have to. I know there won't be anything to find anyway."

As I'm leaving her office, a twelve-year old kid comes up to me and says, "I know you wouldn't do anything like that. You're a great person and I hope you find the person who did this to you."

"Did you show Kim the flyer on Thursday?"

"Yes, I did. Do you know who did this to you?"

"I don't know who did this but it's like an April Fools' joke. Sometimes when people pull pranks, they go too far. This person who pulled the prank wasn't thinking clearly. Everything is going to be fine."

That's what I told him. But I knew, in the long run, it wouldn't be fine. Just like any other situation I've been in; I never let anyone see how things really bother me. I keep things to myself because I know that no matter what I go through, I have to get through it by myself.

176

I couldn't sleep for days. I didn't understand why anyone would want to do this to me. Why would any one person want to try to destroy a person's life like this? I couldn't come up with any legitimate answers. It had to have been someone with no life; someone who was crazy enough to try and ruin somebody else's.

Deep down it was bothering me. But I'm not one to be depressed in front of people. I've always been known to have a smile on my face, even through everything I've dealt with. In the past and even now, I find a way to pull through. Five days after the flyer is discovered Damien sends me an email.

> Frank,
>
> Attached is a poem by Rudyard Kipling called "IF". It was Reggie Lewis' favorite poem, and was read at his funeral. It is also one of my favorite poems, and one that I read whenever things get crazy, when I feel I am being screwed with.
>
> Keep in mind: while we are being quiet, I still support you. Keep your pride, keep your dignity, keep your head up and most of all, keep your sense of humor. Just ignore it and it will eventually go away.
>
> Damien

I can't believe Damien sent a poem. It just shows how sensitive he really is. What am I going to do with a poem?

Once Damien found out about the flyers, he suggested that I tell the lawyer of the league, Sam. Sam used to coach in this league and even though he is a full-time lawyer at his practice, he likes to add his two cents in any situation because the power gets to him and he feels that everyone should listen to him.

I thought to myself, it would be great to have someone close, who knows of the situation, to help me through this matter. I've got nothing to lose; he could give me an insight on how to handle this matter appropriately.

Damien gives me Sam's number and I call him right away.

"Sam, Damien wanted me to give you a call and see what you can do to help me with the crime that has been committed on me."

"Frank, can you tell me why someone would want to do this?"

After telling my story so many times over the weekend, it's becoming a broken record each time everyone asks me. I'm getting to the point that it's becoming tiresome repeating myself every day.

I tell him my story and who I know is behind this. At the conclusion of our conversations he states: "We should sit down and talk about this further. I would like to ask you more questions pertaining to the flyers."

"Sure, it's not a problem. We can meet at any point this week. I'm available in the mornings."

"I'll give you a call sometime this week, to sit down and talk about your situation."

Days go by and Sam never calls me to set up a meeting. I tried calling him, but to no avail. I leave a message, I tell him I'm trying to find out who did this and that it would be greatly
178

appreciated if we could get to the bottom of it. Sam never calls me back. If he doesn't want to get involved then I don't need him to help me.

Just a week after the flyer, Nathan sends an email. It's just one of the many signs that Nathan runs the league. The email should be coming from Damien, but Nathan constructed it. He wants to make sure that Damien gets credit for it even though everyone knows that Damien has nothing to do with it. The email states:

The following is a message which Damien has asked that I forward to the Board.

To the Board of Directors:

As you may know there are postings going up around town accusing Frank Grover of inappropriate behavior. The league and Frank have been in contact with the police and the police have no basis to believe what is in the postings. In fact, the police are actually looking for evidence of who is posting these signs. A lot of coaches and league people are justifiably outraged for Frank and the league shares this with him. On the other hand, the league and the police want to investigate this matter in an appropriate way. Our best approach is to be calm. We will keep you posted as information develops.

Damien

First of all, there are only twenty-two members on the Board of Directors, myself included. This email went out to over thirty recipients; some of which do not belong on the board, but the league was too lazy to figure out who's not affiliated with the league anymore. Now more people who live in other cities are aware of something that, if it wasn't for the email, they wouldn't know what was going on and since the email wasn't specific, I can only imagine the questions that may be asked regarding the flyers.

I never discuss my personal life with anyone else. It seems like the league chose to go the other way and start to peak those unaware of the situation to start asking questions pertaining to the flyer.

Great job if I don't say so myself.

Sam and I never got together. Once I told him who the detective was, he decided to never get involved with me again. So after weeks of trying to talk to him, I gave up on him because to me, it seemed like he never cared; after all, he wasn't gaining anything from me. Knowing that I was a man with very little money, I felt that he didn't want to work on this case because he didn't want to work for nothing. Earning money was more important to him than trying to help a fellow coach who was defamed by cowardly acts.

Two weeks pass and it's time for the annual baseball banquet. Because of the flyers, the league is on high security. Since the person who put up the flyers copied the pictures from the website, he may have also been aware of where the banquet was taking place. Rodney and fellow coaches take turns going out into the parking lot to see if the assailant will put flyers on the vehicles in the parking lot. The league wants to prevent any person who is unaware of the flyers to see them. The league is also afraid for my safety.

Throughout the night, I'm nervous because this is the first time I am with my baseball family since the flyer was distributed. I am unsure who knows about the flyer and if anyone has the wrong perception of me. I do my best not to worry about what may be happening outside but it just doesn't seem possible.

I ask Mr. Baseball, Rodney, and the rest of the coaches if they have seen anything after they've taken their turns watching the parking lot. 'Nothing out of the ordinary' is the usual response. By the end of the night, we, the Giants, receive the playoff championship trophy. The entire night consists of anxiousness, but at least it ends on a bright note.

CHAPTER TWENTY-SEVEN

Shortly after the flyer incident, I pick up a part-time job at a local convenience store chain, Mancini's. I can use the extra money, plus it helps to take my mind off the depressing experience from last month. After hearing from the police that they are at a dead end, I can't sleep any easier, but I try to focus on my life.

I'm still in school full-time and working two jobs. I'm doing as much as I can to keep my mind off of what was done to me. I'm still bothered that someone is getting away with defaming me, but I'm moving on as best as I can.

No one understands what I've been through. I received constant looks of familiarity in the city while taking the train. For the most part, the passengers on the train couldn't pin point where they had seen me before. For months, there would always be someone who would stare at me with a, 'you look familiar and I'm trying to remember how I know you' look. Sometimes after the feeling that I was constantly being watched some people would look at me and ask: "You look familiar, do I know you?"

"I'm sorry but I've never met you before. I tend to get that a lot these days."

"Ok, sorry to bother you."

I have a pretty good memory when it comes to meeting someone; however, the names tend to slip my mind. If they are not important to me, then I won't remember their name. If we played football, hung out, went to parties throughout the years then I would remember, but if they were just a constant face in a place with very minimal interaction with me, I never remember their name.

For months after the flyer came out, I was a constant rider at the Red Line. I didn't feel safe no matter where I was in the city, but that didn't stop me from doing my normal activities. I was working diligently to find the evidence behind this defamation to bring the culprit to justice. I strongly believed I knew who was behind it. Deep down inside it was clearly someone with an affiliation with my ex-girlfriend. My mind was made up with the information that I had witnessed and gathered through Ben and other incidents that seemed subtle to everyone else, but to me were clear cut.

After a couple months of investigating, the police were able to pull finger prints from the flyers but they did nothing after that. There were fingerprints on all the flyers, which should be significant evidence in itself; however the detective leading the investigation told me that the culprit has yet to be discovered. The detective told me that they could not find any camera surveillance showing anyone posting up these flyers.

I found this very interesting. How could someone post up flyers all over the city and not get caught? I could clearly see cameras in the vicinity of many flyers when I retrieved them. It was very odd to me that there wasn't anyone found on camera posting these flyers. Many of the locations had video surveillance, and none of them seemed to work? I didn't believe that at all. But that's what the detective said, so what else was I supposed to do?

The only thing that was discovered was that my ex-girlfriend, Lisa, is a felon. She has a record, but the finger prints on the flyers did not match hers. If I had known she was a felon before, I probably would have handled many things differently. I do believe that if people make mistakes they can learn from them. However, if people make the same mistake twice, I believe that they'll keep making those mistakes. If Lisa was a repeat offender, and I don't know if that was the case, I would not have gone into a relationship with her. People do change, that I do believe, but to what degree is unknown. Am I naïve to think she wasn't involved? I don't know what to believe anymore.

I knew deep down that she didn't post them, but I wasn't completely confident that she was not part of it to begin with.

With Ashley being in his sixties and knowing that he had connections within the city, it would've helped him fight anything illegal that he might've been involved in. He tried his best to make me quit my job and my volunteer work as a coach. I did not quit my job or my volunteer work coaching in Cambridge. I know

Ashley is behind this, I just have to wait for someone to tell me that he's been caught.

I am sitting in the front row of my Sociology class, which is where I sit each and every time because I want to make sure I can pay as much attention as I can. I want to do well in every class, and I don't care that people say only nerds sit in the front. I have a reason to do well.

Professor Wright is a 6' 6" African-American, well-toned individual with a pearly white smile. It was the first thing I noticed about him last year. His teeth are straight and perfect. At the end of the class, Professor Wright approaches me.

"Frank, can I see you before you leave?"

The subtle but clear question is puzzling to me. While I gather my notebook and textbook into my backpack, I'm running through scenarios in my head of why he wants to see me. I know that I'm doing well, maybe not as good as the first six weeks of the semester, but I know I'm hanging in there. I know leading up to this I have no worse than a B in the class. But when the flyers came out, I couldn't focus that much on my school work. I tried but I couldn't give it my all. My attention was focused on trying to find ways to catch Ashley. I was constantly looking at my phone waiting for a phone call or an email stating that they have him in custody. I would look at my phone countless times during the course of day, in class, at work, everywhere I would be. It became a habit I couldn't break from. Realizing this could be why the professor wants to talk to me, I'm ready to tell him about what has been going on in my life. I haven't told many people, my family doesn't even know what's going on. Only the people within the City of Cambridge have any inclination of what's going on with my life at this time. And I didn't even tell them, the league did.

I put on my backpack and I walk towards his desk. He is looking down, reading homework that we have passed in today; I break his concentration, "Professor, you wanted to see me?"

"Yes Frank, I do want to see you. I'm just wondering if you're ok. Your grades have been declining. I know it's only one test and a few homework assignments, but this isn't you. You are also falling asleep in class which is very uncommon and I'm starting to get concerned about you. For the first six weeks, you were happy-go-lucky, with a great attitude, you did well on your tests and homework, and now, for the past couple of weeks, you have done a complete 180."

"You were in my psychology class last year and you did very well. I know something is bothering you. If you want to talk about it, it might help. But if you don't, that's fine. I completely understand and I won't force you to say anything if you don't want to."

I'm debating whether or not I want to tell him. I'm a private person and this event has been very detrimental to me in so many aspects. But now, with the background he has in psychology, it was inevitable that he would notice something was different. He is the only person who has noticed something is wrong or at least he's the first to mention it. I guess it can't hurt to tell him.

"Honestly professor, I am bothered by an event that occurred a few weeks ago, and I'm trying to handle it as best as I

186

can. For the most part, I'm able to hide how I really feel to those around me. You're the first person to mention that I'm not acting the same, I guess I'm not hiding it that well from you."

"Would you like to talk about it?"

I don't say another word. I take off my backpack, swing the backpack forward, open the front pocket and take out the flyer. As I am unfolding it, I look at it, reading what's on the flyer again, not wanting to show him. I say to myself, it can only help. Now he'll understand why I've been different in class these past few weeks.

My hand is shaking as I hand him the flyer. He stands up to read it. As he is reading it, his facial expression says it all. He puts his left hand on his face, in a surprised manner. He pulls out his chair and sits back down. This is something everyone has to sit down for.

"How are you doing? Are you ok?"

"I'm doing the best that I can."

"Do you know who did this to you?"

"I am confident enough to say yes, but the police have yet to find the culprit."

"Well, if you need someone to talk to, I'm here anytime. I hope they catch this person for you."

"Thanks Professor, I appreciate it."

Usually in class, I never hesitate to answer questions, read a paragraph in the book or even give my opinion about what we are being taught and how to perceive it. Ever since the flyers, I secluded myself from answering any questions. I kept quiet, not because I wanted to, but because I was trying to figure out how I can catch the criminal myself after the dead end we have come to.

My sociology professor, just weeks after the flyers came out, noticed a change in my attentiveness. Obviously my attention was directed elsewhere other than school, but he wasn't sure what was bothering me.

Now he knows.

The semester is almost over. I have mustered through it somehow. It wasn't my best semester but I kept going. Day in and day out I still stay positive as much as I can. I still haven't told anybody else about what has happened to me.

Professor Wright must have taken my traumatic event into account when giving me my final grade. It was my best grade of the semester. He gave me a B+. The Professor knew what I was going through and seeing how well I did last year and in the beginning of this semester; he understands the potential I have when I'm at my best. For my other grades, I ended up with a C+ in World Civic I, a C in US History I and a withdrawal in College Writing II. It was by far the worst semester I have ever had since I started at Bunker Hill back in the fall of 2008. Even with the tough road I had this past semester, I signed up for classes in the upcoming semester: College Trigonometry, Literature in America I, World Civic II and Astronomy.

For months I couldn't sleep. I would sometimes be up for a couple days in a row. I would be lucky if I was able to sleep for more than a couple of hours at a time. I typically never sleep for long, four or five hours a night. It's what I've been used to for many years. But during these past few months, I couldn't even get that.

At the O'Brien school, where I work, there would be times I would fall asleep when I was sitting down.

One day Kim comes up to me with a concerned look.

"Frank, you've been dozing off during work. We are all getting worried about you."

"I'm just tired. This semester is just about over and I'll be fine." Kim didn't know that I dropped two classes, Literature in America I and College Trigonometry. I will focus on just two classes. The fewest amount of classes I've taken in any semester. Everything was starting to catch up to me. My restless nights, my countless nightmares, and Ashley yet to be arrested made me lose my motivation. My interest in things was slowly fading and there was nothing I could do to fix it. I just didn't have the energy anymore. Although I knew telling Kim that it was just school and all the hours I'd been working, it was just a scapegoat for how I was really doing. It would just be something temporarily to make them think I was fine. That's what I told her. She believed it. She just thought I was working a lot of hours between two jobs and going to school and it was making me tired.

On any given day, with any other person, that might've been the case. But with me, it was being up all day and night trying to move on with my life, but I couldn't shake it. I needed closure with the one person who had done me wrong.

CHAPTER TWENTY-EIGHT

Just three months after being hired by Mancini's, they want to have a meeting with me. The meeting is with Stephen, the manager of the store and the district manager, Miranda. I'm not sure why they want a meeting, I've done everything right. I don't call out sick. The last time I called out of work was when I was eighteen and my friends stayed over and we pulled an all-nighter. They pressured me to call out early in the morning and that was the last time I called out of work. I felt bad calling out of work that day. Since then I haven't called out sick in ten years.

On a Wednesday morning, Miranda comes into the store and asks Stephen if the three of us can talk. Stephen reassures Miranda that there's another associate working the register and it shouldn't be a problem. As we walk towards the back of the store, there isn't anyone around and Miranda starts the conversation.

"Frank, you have done an exceptional job. Stephen has told me much about you and how quickly you have learned everything here. Having said that and with a new store opening right down the street, we would like to train you to become the assistant manager for that store or even this one. But regardless of the location, we want to promote you."

I am excited to hear this news, but it's no surprise to me that I'm doing well. No matter what I've done in the past, I always find a way to pick up things quickly. When it comes to hands on work, properly trained, I pick things up quite well. But when I'm being taught by reading a manual or by being told how to do something without seeing it physically, I tend to get lost. I'm being promoted to an assistant manager position with only being here for a few months.

"That's great, when do I start training?"

"You will start training here, with Stephen, on learning how to handle the cash and the protocol to follow on a daily basis. However, when we hire assistant managers or managers we train them at our corporate location within a month from their hire or promotion. We will keep in contact to let you know when the next class will take place. It's a week-long extravaganza and the information is critical to know to be the manager we would expect of you."

"That's great to know! I appreciate it very much! Just let me know when it is and I'll be ready for it."

"I will, from what your manager has told me about your performance in so little time, I already know you'll do well in this company."

"Thanks Miranda, I appreciate it a lot. You have no idea how much this helps me."

Stephen and Miranda have no idea what obstacles I have endured this past year and they don't need to know. I've done a great job hiding how greatly affected I am by such heinous events. I always hide things that bother me. I've been like this since I was a little boy; that is how I will always be.

I still can't sleep and my schedule is constantly changing. Working overnights, days, nights and with school work, my brain is in overdrive trying to keep up with everything. I can barely hang in there with my school work. With two jobs and coaching on the horizon in a few weeks, I have to try and compose myself. I don't want anyone to see how much the events have taken their toll on me. I'm not one to show signs of weakness. I am always smiling. My bright personality creates such a positive domino effect for everyone around me, and that's what I'm known for.

School is almost over, even though it is only two classes, it is more than enough at this point in my life. When I receive my grades for the semester, it shows a B+ and a B-. As I look down further, I see an F. How did I get an F in a class I don't remember signing up for? Somehow I signed up for it and now my GPA is affected greatly by the F. I can't remember ever getting an F before, but I did this time. I couldn't focus on school anymore. I didn't sign up for another class. There was no point in doing so if I couldn't focus. All I could think about was trying to find evidence that would nail Ashley down so I can have some closure. I will never sue, I just want an apology. Suing people affects everyone else in this world and no one deserves to be punished for other people's mistakes.

CHAPTER TWENTY-NINE

Six months have gone by since the flyers have been posted all over the city. It will be my first year coaching since the flyers were posted. I'm curious to see if there will be any residual effects caused by them. I haven't dealt with anything or anyone saying anything about the flyers. Some parents would ask me if I'm doing ok. I told them I was, because even if I told them I wasn't, I knew they couldn't do anything about it. I've learned from my past that there isn't anyone who can help, I will get through it as best as I can, on my own.

I will still be able to coach without a scheduling conflict. Right now I'm working two jobs and mentoring Larry's son. He and his wife were looking for someone who can help him with his homework, and he's been looking up to me as a big brother for the past few years. They know about the flyer and the absurdity it proclaims. It is just another thing to prove the skeptics wrong in my eyes. It keeps me busy. I've been working every day since

I've been promoted to an Assistant Manager. I work every afternoon at the O'Brien School, plus I work anywhere between forty to fifty hours a week at Mancini's. At least with being so busy, I am able to keep my mind off the troubling defamation.

People say keeping busy tends to prevent the mind from wandering and thinking too much. So far that's been the case. I don't think too much about it and I haven't encountered any residual effects from the flyer up to this point.

I am walking into the O'Brien school gym for the spring tryouts and a few coaches come over to greet me. Mr. Baseball is the first to reach me and says, "How are you holding up?"

"I'm doing as well as I can."

No one is aware that it has scarred me deeply inside. The smile I fake around everybody is the only way I know how to hide that it bothers me.

Mr. Baseball's assistant walks over to me and says, "I've dealt with crazy women before, but this woman has gone to a new low."

"Honestly, I don't think it was her. I believe it was her crazy ex-boyfriend who she got back together with for a brief time before she started to see Ben's new coach, Johnnie. I have no idea who she's with now and I don't care."

Adam approaches to shake my hand.

Before I can say anything, he says, "What have you been up to this past winter? You weren't hanging with any little children unsupervised were you?" As he pats my back, he quickly says, "I'm just kidding but I'm sure you know that."

It wasn't funny to me. It is a serious matter for someone to joke about.

I laughed at his comment because it was the only way I knew how to handle it. If he knew that his comment bothered me or that I didn't like it, he would make the situation even worse. I wouldn't be surprised if he was a bully back in his teenage years, but now he tries to joke about things that may be serious to someone else. I didn't like it one bit, but as I've learned before, it's best not to make a situation worse so I let him continue his offensive jokes.

I completely understand trying to make light of any situation, but joking about it in the way that the parents and coaches are starting to do, is offensive to me. As I am, I don't let it bother me to the point that I should speak up. I know I should, but what's the point? I'm worried that it will just make the situation worse. Since this happened to me in the past, I know that if you speak up when being bullied, it always seems to make the situation intensify. That is why I am a quiet, reserved person about what happens to and around me.

I don't know what I can do. Nobody understands how much of an impact these flyers could have on my life in the future. For the time being, it's just verbal jokes. I can handle that, for now...

CHAPTER THIRTY

I've been at Mancini's for eight months now. Although I am the assistant manager, I convinced my manager to hire Aaron as an associate; he is picking things up very quickly. Aaron adapts quite well to the lottery machine, which is typically the hardest thing for people to learn.

On his third day of training, I leave to go to the bank and deposit the daily cash and grab a bite to eat. Just as I'm about to order the food to go, Aaron calls me.

"Frank, I think I made a mistake."

"What happened?"

"A guy came in and he won money on the daily number game. The machine flashed the amount he won and I grabbed the cash from the drawer. I gave him his ticket back because he had more drawings on the ticket."

"Did another ticket print?"

"Yes it did and I gave it to him."

"Ok, so what's the problem?"

"I think I hit clear instead of accept on the lottery machine and before I knew it, he was gone and I already gave him the money."

"Ok, I'll be back soon and I'll try and figure it out."

I arrive back to work and I head into the office to take a look at the video surveillance. It was clear that Aaron made the mistake by giving the customer the winning ticket back and not hitting accept on the lottery machine.

I call my manager and ask him if there is something I can do about it.

"How much was it for?"

"The ticket was worth $228.00."

"There are a couple of things you can do. You can fire him since it was a big mistake with cash or have him pay it out of pocket and chop it up as a personal loss."

I'm not going to fire my friend, not unless I know he did something wrong on purpose. I partially blame myself for the situation that has occurred. I leave the office and have a talk with Aaron.

"Aaron, we have a few choices. I could fire you, but I'm not going to do that. I know it was an honest mistake and I blame myself for not teaching you that aspect of the lottery machine. We are a new store and it doesn't happen that often. Do you have the money now to fix the mistake?"

"No, I just started."

"I know that but I just have to make sure. This is what I'll do. I'll put in the money myself and when you get the chance, you can pay me back. I'm not worried about it right now. I'm going to make another phone call to Stephen and see what he has to say about it."

If it wasn't Aaron, I wouldn't let anyone else borrow the money. The associate would have had two options: to be fired or to pay it back immediately. But because I have known Aaron for six years, I knew that I could trust him to pay me back.

I call Stephen and let him know the situation.

"Frank, you can call Tom at the lottery headquarters and explain to him what happened. He might be able to let you know if there's something else you can do."

Stephen gives me the phone number. I call Tom right away.

"Hello, this is Tom."

"Hi Tom, this is Frank Grover and I am the assistant manager for Mancini's in Everett. I have a situation and I was told to talk to you in regards to it."

"Yes, Frank. Tell me what happened."

I told him the story of how Aaron made the mistake on the lottery machine.

"There is something you can do, but it doesn't guarantee anything."

"What can we do?"

"You have to write down exactly what happened and how it happened. You have to state how much it was for, what game it was from and at what time and why the situation occurred. Then you need to sign and date it and fax it over to me and we will make a decision here at the office and contact you regarding the matter."

"Ok Tom, I thank you for your time and I will send it to you later today. Thanks again."

I hang up the phone and I go back to Aaron to tell him what happened.

"Aaron, Tom said we might be able to get it credited to our daily lottery sales. But for the time being, we will have to go about it as if you owe me the money until we hear otherwise."

"Ok, Frank. Thanks for letting me know."

The next day I notice on the daily lottery sales from the previous day that it shows a $228.00 surplus. Tom never called me back to state it was credited to the account but since it was, I told Aaron about the decision the lottery made and we no longer have to worry about the money. It made his day; he was getting ready to pay me back with the money he borrowed from his father.

CHAPTER THIRTY-ONE

In May 2010, I decide to tell my mother about the flyer. She's always been there for me. Seven months have passed since the flyer and I feel that she needs to know. She's working for my Aunt Tracy today. She helps my aunt on the days she has off from her regular job. I'm going to stop by and tell her.

As I arrive at my aunt's store, there isn't a customer around. It is perfect timing for a talk. I head into the office. Both my mother and my aunt are there.

"Ma, I have something to tell you."

"What? Are you having a kid?"

"No, I wish it was that. It's not a good thing."

"Someone put up a flyer about me last year and I thought you should know about it just in case you don't hear it from me first."

"What are you talking about?"

I take out the flyer and show it to her.

"Do you know who did this?"

"Yeah, I know who did this. I've gone to the police and right now they say we are at a dead end."

"Was this Lisa?"

"No Ma, it wasn't Lisa but I believe it was her ex-boyfriend."

"Who is this fucking guy? I want to rip his fucking balls off!"

My mother gives my Aunt the flyer.

"When did this happen?"

"It happened last October during Columbus Day weekend."

"Why would anyone want to do this?"

"I have no idea."

I wanted my mother to know before Jack or anyone else told her. I would rather have the news come from me first. I'm surprised it has lasted this long without my mother finding out. But since we are in the midst of the season, I knew word would soon spread quickly. I leave my aunt's store and head over to Comeau field for our practice.

With Jim's mom and Andre's father being added to the staff this year, it gives us five coaches. We are able to split up duties accordingly: pitching coach, hitting coach, bench coach and fielding coach. I manage the game at hand and prepare the lineups, the pitching scenarios, and any situational plays that may occur. Aaron would coach third base and Cedric; who was added to the Giants staff last year when Jack left, is coaching first base. Jim's mom would get the bench going. Andre's father would work on baseball mechanics since he understands the science of baseball. He was also a great athlete in college. I manage everything else by gathering opinions and making timely decisions, like any manager would do.

This year Eddie breaks his ankle before the start of the baseball season, he will be out for most of the year and possibly the playoffs. He is our starting pitcher and a great offensive weapon. It's just another obstacle to try and overcome in this baseball world.

The Giants' players thought we couldn't be a great team without him. It would be difficult trying to win games without one of the best players on the team, and as a coaching staff, we knew it would make it difficult to go to the Mayor's Cup this year. However, we also knew that this would give us the opportunity to see what we were capable of without Eddie.

Coaching this year, outside of working, comforts me more than anything else. I am able to hang out with my friends and talk about baseball, movies, and reminisce about the previous seasons we've coached. The predictions coaches make prior to the beginning of the season and then seeing the end results is something I look forward to every year. Every night there's a few of us that gather together behind the field. I've called this the Coaches' Corner for many years now, and we talk about the season, the teams we have and how some coaches lost games and how others impress us on certain situations. It brings calmness to the events that I've dealt with. I didn't think I would enjoy coaching much this year, but it turns out to be the one thing that has helped me through the process.

We finish the season with a 3 – 13 record. Eddie comes back from his injury during the last week of the season; right in time to scrape off whatever rust he might have before the playoffs. It wasn't a frustrating season because I knew it was going to be a tough year since Eddie broke his ankle. I knew we weren't the strongest team, but we always went into every game knowing that we had a chance.

The playoffs are about to start and the Cardinals are the #1 seed in the playoffs, we are the 4th seed.

Before the game starts, Eddie and Scott approach me. Scott was my first pick last fall and he's our primary catcher.

"Hey Coach, we saw a flyer with your picture on it."

"Where did you find it?"

"It was on a pole in front of Lindstrom field on the other side of Cambridge."

"Is it true?"

"No guys, it's not true. Someone was trying to pull a prank and that person went too far. If you do find anymore I need to know."

"Sure Coach. We'll let you know."

"Thanks Scott. Go warm up Eddie, he's pitching today."

As they go to warm up, I step away from the field and call Detective Douglas. I leave a voice mail since he doesn't pick up and then send him an email regarding the incident.

In the 5th inning, during a very competitive game, there is a play at the plate. Our starting catcher Scott has played almost every game this season in this position. He protects the plate by putting his left foot in front of it to block the runner from trying to score.

As the throw comes in from second base, the runner slides feet first into the catcher's leg. The dirt comes up from the slide blocking my point of view. The umpire calls safe. Scott never catches the ball. He's down on the ground in significant pain.

After a fifteen minute delay, I have to make a change at the catcher's position. Scott is now out with a broken ankle. Just our luck, one player breaks his ankle before the season and comes back for the playoffs, and another player breaks his ankle in the playoffs and is out for the remainder of the year.

We eventually lose 8 to 6. I know the players will be down from losing our starting catcher for the playoffs. I'm not a person who speaks well in public. But when I do have something important, something on my mind, I'm not afraid to go all out. I feel that now isn't the best time to have a postgame speech. There's nothing we can do since it's over. I have to wait for the beginning of the next game to do it. I have to give one of my best speeches in order to revive any motivation that is quickly dwindling with the players. A speech that will give something that will be memorable and hopefully create the willpower to fight through with all the obstacles we have overcome this year.

I let the other coaches handle this postgame speech. I chime in on how proud I am of this team being very resilient. But for the most part, which is uncommon for me, I keep relatively quiet. We don't know who we are playing until tomorrow night. There is no need in getting ready for a team that we don't know who we will be playing at this point.

I receive an email from the detective saying that he sent someone over to Lindstrom field but they can't find the flyer. I find it amusing how young kids can find it but the god damn detectives can't. Something doesn't seem right here. I don't believe him. Something is telling me that none of this makes sense.

CHAPTER THIRTY-TWO

It's Friday afternoon and we are gathered at the field to prepare ourselves to play the Astros. If we lose this game we will be eliminated from the playoffs.

I gather everyone to the bench. Before I start my speech, Scott hobbles out of his mother's car with crutches and sits himself on the bench. He has a giant red cast on his leg and before I can say anything he says, "Coach I'm still part of the team, I have to support them any way I can. I tried to get an orange cast, but they didn't have orange."

Everyone knows that my favorite color is orange. In the beginning of the season I asked Mr. Loney if we could get orange jerseys. Not only were we able to get orange jerseys but he ordered orange helmets too. Everyone loves the orange jerseys; even the parents and coaches.

"That's all right Scott, as long as you are doing better, that's all that matters."

Everyone wants to sign the cast. I let them sign the cast first before I start my speech. Once everyone has signed the cast, I make sure they are all sitting down and attentive to what I have to say. The players know better not to talk during our speeches.

Here I go.

"We as a team have been through many obstacles this year. With Eddie breaking his ankle before the season and now Scott with his broken ankle, it doesn't seem like we have the luck this year. Remember one thing though; you only have luck if you believe it. These were unfortunate events that have occurred and for whatever reason, they happened to us this year. I think we had a great regular season. Even though the record doesn't indicate it, you all played hard and played as a team every single game. We had bad breaks, some mental mistakes and a lot of 1-run defeats. If anything, it showed the potential this team has. Let me ask all of you a question, even the coaching staff. Does anyone know who the last team was to win four games in a row and win the playoff championship?"

Everyone looks at one another, not knowing the answer.

"It happened four years ago, in the Majors. It is also the year before I took over the Giants."

Still unsure of the answer, they wait for me.

"It was the Giants of 2006. This team has a history of fighting back with our backs against the wall. The Giants did it in 2006, and we fell just short of it in 2007 when it was my first year as the manager of the Giants. Last year we won the playoffs. This is isn't about what happened last season or even this season. This is about now. You guys have a chance to be a part of history. No team has ever won more games in the playoffs than the regular season. We can be that team. We can win, I know that. You all have to believe we can too."

After the pregame speech ends, I sense urgency within the team. The motivation is back, it's just a matter of doing everything right, at the right time. Cedric says to me after the speech, "That was the best speech you've conducted since I've been here. Not that any of your speeches are bad, this one was clearly thought out. It was impressive if I don't say so myself."

"Thanks Cedric. I felt I had to make sure they knew what was at stake. It's important to me that they understand how a team can win at any point regardless of past experiences, especially if nothing else seems to be going well in the beginning."

"I think your words inspired them. Your words got to me. It was definitely an uplifting speech."

"We will just have to see how much of an effect it has on them going forward."

We beat the Astros in an offensive battle with the score 12 to 10. We survive from being eliminated for at least one more game.

We beat the Cardinals the following game 12 to 1 to make it to the Championship round against the Nationals.

This is our first playoff matchup since Jack has officially taken over the Nationals this year.

Jack's ace is starting this game against our second ace of the team. It's favorable for Jack's team to win. But knowing the control issue Jack's ace can have, I made sure I huddled up the team before the game.

"Listen everyone; we are all aware of Simon's control problems, it will be best for everyone to wait for the first strike call. Once we get his pitch count high, he won't have much left to do. If we are able to have him throw a lot of pitches we will be able to do well once the relievers come in."

In the first inning, Simon throws 30 pitches. Once he throws 85 pitches he's done for the game. If he throws less than 65 pitches he will be able to pitch the next game, if the Nationals were to lose. We are able to get one run during Simon's struggles that 1st inning.

The second inning Simon throws 18 pitches. So far it's going according to our plan. It's just a matter of time before Jack has to make a decision with his pitcher.

The third inning arrives and Simon has a 9 pitch inning. Not what we hoped for but nevertheless the pitch count is getting higher. With 57 pitches, Simon has either 28 to go, or if Jack decides to pull him to save him just in case, it will be 7 more pitches.

In the fourth inning and with us holding a slim 2 – 1 edge, Jack elects to have Simon start this inning. With one out, and in the middle of count, he pulls Simon for another pitcher. Jack decides to hold off on using Simon as much as he can for this game. I thought that this was the best thing for us. Now we have a better chance of winning this game. It also puts us in a greater position to win the championship if we make it to the next game.

The game starts to get out of hand after the pitching change. We win 10 to 2 and we are now one win away from being back to back playoff champions. We are one win away of making an improbable comeback. The momentum has clearly shifted in our favor.

With the Championship game between two old friends about to begin, Jack arrives to the field a little late. He says to me, "Frank, my team gets to pick what dugout; we want the first base side because we are the home team."

"No Jack, you are not the home team today. You were the home team the other day and since we are playing one another again, we are now the home team."

"That's not fair. We are the better ranked team in the playoffs. We should have home field advantage for the whole playoffs."

"That's not true. The rules say otherwise."

"That's bullshit. I'm calling Damien. This is outrageous."

"Go ahead Jack, I'm telling you the truth."

He gets Damien on the phone.

"We should be the home team! We are the best ranked team in the playoffs."

As I hear Jack blasting at Damien over the phone, I work my way over to Mr. Baseball just to confirm what I know.

"Mr. Baseball, we are home today considering they were the home team the last game, right?"

"Yes, you are right."

Jack is creating a scene at this point. His temper is getting the best of him and I've never seen him this angry before. He must've had a bad day at work. He's yelling left and right, in front of all his staff and players. I'm calm, cool and collected as I've always been known to be.

Jack won't even talk to me since he got off the phone with Damien. He knows he was wrong but he won't admit it right now.

I'm watching his team and his players. Already the tension is causing a snowball effect onto his coaching staff and players. Unfortunately for him, it's not how you want to start before the game begins. For us, it can easily be a blessing in disguise.

Jack decides to have Simon pitch the first inning. Simon has 36 pitches left to throw. As the second inning comes to an end, so does Simon's pitching. After that inning, we start to score, and we eventually win 9 – 2. We complete one of the best comebacks that I have ever witnessed in this league. This is the first time that a major league team has won more games in the playoffs than in the regular season.

As we are gathering at home plate for typical good game handshakes/high fives, the coaches are the last to shake hands, and as Jack and I come to one another, he puts his hand down and walks away without acknowledging a good game.

If there's any sign of poor sportsmanship, it's Jack's attitude at this point. There was no reason for him to do what he did, and for all the years we've been friends this was the first time I felt disrespected by him. That was a low blow by my best friend.

I've been through a very tumultuous year in so many ways and I can't deal with my best friend being out of line with me. I know that at this moment, I have a win to celebrate with my team, as back to back playoff champions.

Two years in a row we've won the playoffs. Through the hard times I dealt with personally, this is by far the most rewarding season I've ever been a part of. It has certainly made me forget what I've been through for now. These past two years have been the worst for me personally, but my best two years as a manager. I've always overcome adversity when faced with it. Last year it was Lisa and her constant ranting and raving and trying to cause a scene. This year it was Ashley's flyers that tried to get the best of me. So far, two years with my life personally troubled, my coaching abilities are peaking. Coaching has been my sanctuary. It's the one thing that has taken my mind off things because I'm always talking with my friends when I'm at the field.

After working two jobs for the past eight months, I am finally able to buy a car. My frequent trips on the train will end.

A year has passed since the flyers came out. The culprit has still gotten away with the crime he committed. The first season after the defamation occurred and I survived as best as I could.

Still jokes come and go, and they have dwindled since the flyers first came out, but they still exist. Adam is the main reason the jokes keep happening but other than that, everything seems to be going just fine.

CHAPTER THIRTY-THREE

I am working a Thursday morning shift in early October. Miranda and the Loss Prevention manager, Burt, come in to the store and have a talk with the current manager. After they come out of the meeting, Miranda and Burt approach me.

"Frank, you're going to be the interim manager for now until we figure out what we are going to do. We just fired the manager for logging in false hours."

Just seven months after I was promoted to assistant manager, I've been tossed into the manager position because the previous manager was being stupid. It's another opportunity for me to show the company what I'm capable of doing.

"Ok, Miranda. Is there anything I need to know?"

"Burt will show you some of the surveillance and what to do about certain situations that may arise. But other than that, Colin, the training supervisor, will show you how to handle daily activities next week. We still need to train you at our corporate location. We've neglected you the past few months but you'll be trained. I promise."

"You better keep that promise because I never make one unless I know I'm going to keep it."

"Trust me you'll be in the training class soon. As manager, you need to log in fifty hours every week."

"Ok that's fine, when will I get a pay raise?"

"We will talk in the next week or so to iron out the details. For now, just keep doing the great job you've been doing and we'll talk soon."

"What about an assistant manager?"

"We are going to have someone from another store take care of your days off until we figure something out."

"What about Aaron? I think he will be a good candidate to train as an assistant manager."

"Frank, we will keep that in mind. But for now just go about business and Seika will be filling in for your days off. He has been trained down the street and this gives him more experience for the time being."

"That is fine but I just want you to remember that I think Aaron should be trained as soon as possible."

"One day at a time Frank."

Miranda is getting a little aggravated with my responses. Replacing the manager position is what she is focused on right now and training an assistant for me isn't high on her priority list.

The only one who can cover the store on my days off is another assistant manager from the store down the street. I just can't do all of this myself. I don't trust anyone from another store.

214

I've already taught Aaron some stuff. I know he'll be a manager one day. I know how to run this store. When a different person comes in, it makes a lot of people uncomfortable and I don't like that.

A few weeks pass and I am working sixty plus hours every week as the manager. I still haven't received the manager's pay. I feel like they're using me as much as they can so they can pay me less money for as long as they can. I'm ready to give Miranda my two cents on my pay, how much I have to do, and that I need someone who I know I can rely on. The fill-in assistant manager is making ordering mistakes and doesn't understand the flow of the store. He constantly calls me for questions. I'm always working even when I'm not. If I don't hear from Miranda by December, I will start training Aaron on a daily basis.

I have to work an overnight shift to cover one of my cashiers who called out earlier in the day. Being short staffed, with no reliable assistant manager, it's my responsibility to fill in when there isn't anyone else to cover the shift. We only have one overnight cashier, if we had two it would be easier, but this store doesn't generate enough cash flow yet.

During my shift, around 2:00 in the morning, an African-American male in his mid-twenties about 5' 11" walks into the store. It takes him a couple of minutes to grab a few snacks.

As he approaches the counter, he asks, "Is this store looking to hire anyone?"

"We are accepting applications at this time for part-time help."

"Could I have an application?"

"Yes you can."

I tear an application off and hand him one.

As he is filling out the application, he starts asking questions about the responsibilities of the store and the starting pay.

"It's an easy job to be a cashier here. The only problems that may arise would be robberies or catching someone stealing. For the most part, the hardest thing to learn would be the lottery machine if you don't have any experience with it."

"I don't have experience with the lottery. But everything else seems comparable with the job I currently hold now at a dollar store. By the way I'm Terrance." He introduces himself.

"It's nice to meet you Terrance, I'm Frank."

Terrance and I talk for two hours. He seems like an individual who is really interested in working overnights at my store. I am pleased with Terrance's personality and overall customer service abilities. He is very adamant to work for someone who can give him the hours that he needs and the overnight shift will suit him well. His other job isn't giving him the hours he needs to survive and he could really use another one.

"I'm all set with the application."

"Ok, thanks Terrance."

I'm glancing at the application and before I can look at the back of it, Terrance interrupts me.

"Who should I speak to regarding an opening?"

"Actually, it would be me. I'm the manager at this store."

"Oh, can I call you later this week?"

"Yes, that will be fine. It's pretty busy for me in the beginning of the week. It settles down by Wednesday and I should be able to review your application. If you don't hear from me by Friday, you can call me then."

"Ok, thanks. I'll talk to you later this week."

He leaves the store and I'm able to review the application further. He checked off that he hasn't committed any crimes, he didn't finish high school, and he works at the dollar store not too far from here. I also learn that he used to live in Texas.

I do need to hire someone reliable to take over the overnight shifts in order to have a consistent morning schedule. Terrance seems like a suitable candidate to hire to ease up my schedule a bit.

By Wednesday I am able to finish reviewing Terrance's application. It seems that he is a reliable candidate for the position. I call Terrance later that day and ask him if he can come in for an interview on Friday at noon. He agrees to do so.

On Friday, Terrance arrives and knocks on my office door. I ask him a series of questions pertaining to his past-work experiences, education, how many hours he wants to work, and what his goals would be in working for this company.

I've never interviewed anyone before to work for this company. I used to be a manager in wholesale, so I just ask the generic questions that I've grown accustomed to.

I ask him to fill out other paperwork regarding a background check. I also ask him for his social security card and identification card to make copies.

After waiting from corporate for the go ahead, I am able to hire him for a part-time position. It's all I am able to do at this time since we are a brand new store. Plus, I have a quota of hours to go by each week.

Part-time is considered to be under forty hours, and I'm able to keep him just under that. After a couple of weeks, he has done exceptionally well and Miranda tells me I can give Terrance a full-time position as an Overnight Specialist.

CHAPTER THIRTY-FOUR

A few days ago my Aunt Tracy confided in me about some accounts that she dealt with when she was younger. It is a conversation I will never forget.

"Frank, did you ever find out who put the flyers around town about you?"

"No Auntie, they never caught the criminal even though I know who did it. For some odd reason or another they couldn't find any surveillance footage; even though there are finger prints on the flyer, either Ashley refused to give them up or the cops didn't even bother."

My aunt says to me, "When I was younger, my father molested me. He would do it almost every day until I was able to finally break free. My sister-in-law dealt with it tremendously from her brother. Some of my friends dealt with it as well."

She named people left and right. Most of the people I know, but I didn't need to know what happened to them. She told me anyway. It brought tears to her eyes. I consoled her with a hug and told her that I'm sorry that these events happened to her and everyone else she knows.

"Frank, unfortunately it happened a lot back in the 60's and 70's. It was normal back then."

"It's never normal Auntie."

"That's true, but I just had to tell you because I'm outraged anyone would defame you like that. We all know the kind of person you are and who you're not. I feel your mother's fury closely, as we both want to grab Ashley by the balls and have him feel the pain he's caused you."

My Aunt Tracy talked to me for two hours about this. I never knew this happened to everyone she named. All the people she told me about dealt with the same heinous crime that Ashley accused me of doing towards little kids.

I was upset when I found out that these things happened to them. There was nothing I could do to help them get through that traumatic event, but it helped them to talk to someone about it. Of course I felt distaste for the people who were still alive that did this to my family and friends, but just like everything else, I couldn't do anything. The culprits are covered by the Statute of Limitations on the crimes they committed on my family and friends.

How would my fellow coaches like it if they were in my shoes dealing with this defamation? I know how some of my family and friends feel.

A few days after the conversation that my Aunt Tracy and I had, I have my yearly checkup with my physician.

The doctor comes into the room.

"Hi, Frank." He shakes my hand.

"How have you been feeling lately?"

"Doc, my scalp has been very itchy for almost a year now, and I just don't know what's going on."

He takes a look at my scalp.

"Frank, when did you start having irritation on your scalp?"

"I remember having the irritation since January. I just didn't have any insurance to see anyone about it until now."

"It looks like psoriasis. Did you ever have it before?"

"No doc. This is the first time."

"Did anything happen to you that could cause stress?"

"Yes, about a year ago. Something did happen to me. It was very traumatic."

"It seems that event made you break out with psoriasis. A stressor in life can cause psoriasis to break out like that. How have you been feeling lately?"

"I feel ok. I know I could be better, but I try to move on as best as I can."

After fifteen minutes talking with the doctor, he has come up with two conclusions; he has officially diagnosed me with depression, and he recommends that I see a specialist regarding my psoriasis. Medication was adamantly advised by my doctor to help with the depression. I don't like to take medicine. I don't even like to take aspirin for a headache, let alone any other drug; especially not knowing what the side effects could do to my body. I never filled out the prescription.

CHAPTER THIRTY-FIVE

The preseason practices for the new season of baseball are starting in a month, but I don't know if I can deal with another year of being verbally abused from my colleagues.

I don't know what I can do to fix my depression. I'm usually strong enough but I've succumbed to everything that's been happening to me. It took a year for depression to kick in, or at least that's what I've come to understand. I'm going to stop by to see Professor Wright. He might be able to suggest something for me to do.

I'm waiting patiently for Professor Wright's students to leave his classroom. The door is wide open and he sees me hanging out in the hall. There are still a few students remaining but he waves me into his room regardless. I stand ten feet from his desk waiting for his students to finish up their comments, questions or concerns before I talk to the professor.

He looks over to me as he's answering the students' questions, acknowledging my presence by nodding his head. At that time, I take a seat. As the last student leaves, I stand up. He comes over to me; he shakes my hand and gives me a man hug. A man hug ends with a couple hard pats on the back.

"How are you doing Frank?"

"Honestly, I could be better. It's starting to hit me a lot more these days. I've been diagnosed with depression. I'm wondering if you could suggest something outside the box that could help me through this process."

"Frank, give me more of an insight on what you've been doing lately and maybe I can pinpoint something. I haven't seen you in over a year; I'm guessing some things have changed."

"I'm working seventy to eighty hours a week between two jobs. I'm mentoring a couple's son. They came to me last year and asked if I could help their son because he looks up to me as a big brother. I've known them for four years. Also, coaching is right around the corner. Most importantly, the defamation incident that I talked to you about a year ago was never solved. They never found the person, or as I like to put it, they gave him a slap on the wrist, strictly my opinion. My friends and colleagues of the league would make fun of the flyer. This put me in a position to either tell them it bothered me and face the consequence of it escalating, or laugh with them as if nothing bothered me. So I laughed with them; it was easier because those consequences were predictable. After the flyer came out, my family and friends also put me in a position to listen to them of what happened when they were younger; they were assaulted or molested."

"Frank, no matter the experiences you've dealt with, I commend you for still staying as strong as you are. The majority of people would be very aggressive to the ones that have done them wrong. But you still keep a calm demeanor. Your ability to cope with things is only making you stronger. Even though you've been diagnosed with depression, it's just an obstacle. I know you can fight through it. Staying constantly busy can be a good thing, but it can also be a bad thing. I honestly think you are doing way too much. Your family and friends that have told you about their stories feel more comfortable telling them to you but at the same time, it's not something you want to hear. I would start off by taking a vacation. Get away from everyone and everything. Although you'll think a lot, there's a good chance you'll come to some sort of euphoric realization."

"I can't take a vacation Professor. I have way too much to do. I don't have an assistant manager at work yet, and I just wouldn't be able to leave until I'm comfortable with a reliable assistant manager."

"You're putting too much pressure on yourself. Just by how you've responded, it is obvious that you're in over your head and trying to do too much. If you can't take a vacation now, I suggest you lower you work load. You need time for yourself; you focus too much on everyone and everything else. If you don't take care of yourself, no one will. If you don't do something about your depression now, I'm afraid it will only get worse."

"I guess you're right. Thanks, Professor."

"If you need anything else Frank, you know where I am."

"I know and I appreciate it."

I walk out of the room knowing what I have to do. It's the only way I can try and make sense of things around me, and try to recover from everything I've dealt with. It's time I go talk to Kim. It's the best option for me right now.

I walk into Kim's office at 1:30 pm, a half hour before anyone else would come in.

"Can I talk to you Kim?"

"Is everything alright?"

I close the door.

I grab a chair and sit down ten feet from her desk.

Before I can say a word, I begin to ball my eyes out.

"What's wrong Frank?"

She's never seen me like this before.

"I need a break. I can't do this anymore. There's just so much going on, and no one knows how I feel inside. I can't hide my emotions anymore. It is beating me up inside. There's only so much I can take."

"Is it anyone in particular?"

"It's just everything that has happened to me the past year and a half. I just need to step back. I'm doing way too much."

With tears falling steadily from my eyes, my words burst out in between emotional pauses. "I...I...I... caaaan...caaan caaan't... do... this...I...I...nee...need... a...a...a... bre...bre...break... froooo...frooo...from... thisss."

She comes over and hugs me as tears start to fall from her eyes.

In the seven years that she's known me, she has never seen me like this before. No one has. I never cry.

"Sure, if that's what you need. I'll call the office and just tell them you're taking a leave of absence."

I try to gather myself before anyone else comes in.

"Thanks."

I leave before anyone else can see me like this. I don't want anyone else to know there's something wrong.

CHAPTER THIRTY-SIX

Four weeks go by and I've been focusing on my full-time job. I can't remember the last time I had a day off to do absolutely nothing. For two years I was going nonstop thinking it would be beneficial. During these past four weeks I've had days off to relax. I have always been busy with something; working, doing homework, coaching, working at the afterschool program, and mentoring. Now all I've been doing is working my full-time job. Coaching is right around the corner, but for once in a long time I'm busy for just fifty hours a week. This has been relaxing for me in a way I never thought it would be.

February starts practice for the upcoming season and the gym would be available to use after school vacation. I made the necessary phone calls to designate practice that would take place on Fridays at the O'Brien School.

During the practices I held, I wasn't enjoying myself. I designated my assistants to conjure up drills inside the gym.

Fortunately for me, I have four reliable assistant coaches who took over when my head wasn't in the baseball mood. I tried my best to be in the mood as much as I could, but no matter what I tried, I just couldn't. I could hide it well, but not well enough without two people noticing.

I only told two people about my depression; Jim's mom and her husband. I've known them for six years. They noticed a change of behavior in me that for the most part was unnoticeable. For the few who knew me, and knew me well, they were the only ones that noticed that there was something wrong with me. Jim's father was also dealing with depression. They expressed their concern for me.

In March, I went back to work at the afterschool program. After a six week leave, I believed it was time to go back but only for a couple days a week. I can't work seventy plus hours anymore. I have restricted my work week to fifty-eight hours by working just Wednesdays and Fridays at the afterschool program. I feel great, well better anyway. There are people who saw the difference in me from January to now. I'm not 100% but I'm getting there.

On my first day back at the afterschool program, a ten-year old kid runs up to me. He puts his hands around me and gives me a hug. Kim sees what this kid is doing. I raise my hands straight-up in the air. I wasn't going to hug him back.

He looks up to me and says, "I thought you left. Where did you go?"

"Jonathan, I had to take a break. I had to deal with some things of my own."

"I'm glad you're back. No one else will play sports with us. Every other teacher just watches us. But you play with us and you make it more fun for us."

"Well Jonathan, I'm back. But I'll only be here two days of the week. I have a job that's more important than this one that I have to concentrate on."

CHAPTER THIRTY-SEVEN

As I come into work Thursday morning, I see Terrance smoking a cigarette outside.

"Terrance can you please clean up this lot, it is a mess."

"Sure thing boss, Frank, when are we going to hang out?"

For the longest time Terrance has been begging me to hang out with him. I was busy in the past. Only working fifty-eight hours a week has taken quite a bit off my normal workload.

"We can, if you'd like. I was pretty busy in the past. I didn't have an assistant manager, but now Aaron is capable of doing it on his own. I'm actually free on Saturday afternoon if you are."

Aaron could take care of the daily audit on his own. I feel comfortable enough that he can do it without any problems. He's a smart kid, plus Saturdays are one of the easiest days to do a daily audit.

"Yeah, Saturday sounds like a great day for me too!"

"Ok, let's plan for Saturday afternoon. Say one?"

"Yes. That'll be great!"

Two days pass.

I am on my way to pick up Terrance when I receive a phone call from Aaron.

"Frank, I don't know what I did wrong but there's a $355.00 discrepancy. I looked it over a few times and I can't figure it out for the life of me."

"Are all the numbers in the correct slots; lottery fund, cash, coupons, ATM fund, etc.?"

"Yes, all the numbers are in the right spot. I checked all three shifts and I can't figure out why our cash is $355.00 short."

"Ok, I'll swing by before Terrance and I head out to lunch."

"Ok, Thanks."

The audits have to be done by noon, but considering it was a Saturday, there wasn't anybody in the corporate office so we have some leeway to finish it up.

I arrive at Terrance's apartment at 12:30 and I knock on the door. He opens the door with excitement and says, "I'm ready, let's go. It's been a while since I've gone out with any friends."

"Aaron needs me to stop by the store so I can help him sort out a problem first, and then we can be on our way."

"Sure, it's not a problem."

As I am driving down route 16 in Everett, Terrance turns to me and says, "Can we stop by Dunkin Donuts to grab a coffee?"

"Yeah, sure, I'll grab one as well."

I only drink iced coffee. We don't have an iced coffee machine at my store. I always stop by Dunkin Donuts in the morning because I never have time to go to Mary Lou's in Quincy. Mary Lou's coffee is my weekend treat to myself. It's a fifteen mile drive one way for it, but it is well worth the drive each and every time.

Terrance and I decide to go through the drive thru, which I really never like to do because I can't watch how they pour my coffee. I'm very particular with my coffee; just my coffee, nothing else. Since Terrance begged me to go to the drive thru, I have to trust the cashier to make it right this time. It is usually hit or miss with Dunkin Donuts these days.

As the cashier hands me Terrance's hot coffee; the lid comes off and the boiling hot coffee spills all over my lap. I know things like this happen all the time so I don't get upset with the cashier.

"This is why I like to go in Terrance. I don't mind waiting in a line for a coffee."

As I point towards the glove compartment I ask, "Terrance can you grab me some napkins?"

He opens the glove compartment and as he's grabbing some napkins, flyers drop onto the floor of the car.

"What's this?"

"It's a long story, but the bottom line is, a man was trying to defame me for something I didn't do. I've kept the flyers for evidence in case he commits another crime. The cops told me to throw them out but I didn't want to. It just seemed odd that the police wanted me to get rid of evidence.

232

"It says that you sold drugs to children and that you molested them."

"I know what it says. It's all lies because some sixty year old bastard had nothing better to do than try and ruin my reputation. Nothing came out of it because it was all false. The police looked into the matter and didn't find any accusations regarding the crimes it proclaimed I did. They know it was just someone defaming me."

"That's pretty serious stuff. Why would anyone do that to you?"

"Honestly, I have no idea. Some people are just rude bastards. But it didn't prevent me from continuing coaching or working at an after-school program. It's a long story and I just don't want to explain it. Please put the flyers back in the glove compartment."

Terrance puts the flyers back in the compartment and nothing else is said of the matter. I pull into the parking lot of my store. I have to try and figure out what Aaron did wrong, if anything.

"Terrance, do you want to stay in the car or do you want to come in? It shouldn't take me long to figure out."

"I'll just stay here."

"Ok, not a problem. I should only be ten to fifteen minutes."

I walk into the store and there's a cashier at the desk.

"Even on your days off, you come in." The cashier says.

"This is my store. I have to make sure everything is running right. I like to surprise my cashiers from time to time just to make sure they are doing their job."

Every cashier knows by now that I like to stop in unannounced. As long as everything is going good, my time spent at the store decreases. I very rarely come when Aaron is working. But when he's not working, I make a surprise visit when I'm in the area.

I walk into the office. "Ok Aaron, what did you do wrong?"

He senses my sarcasm.

"Real funny Frank, I told you, I double checked everything and couldn't find a mistake anywhere."

"I bet you lunch that I will notice something you did wrong. If I don't see a mistake you made, I owe you lunch."

"Alright, you're on."

Fifteen minutes pass.

"So Frank, I expect Wendy's Monday afternoon."

"Not so fast Aaron. I think I see the issue."

He's new at this position so I expect him to make a mistake somewhere. It might seem like a big mistake to him but it wasn't to me.

I have figured out the problem.

"Aaron, your dyslexia kicked in." I say jokingly.

"What do you mean?"

"Instead of putting $482.00 in a slot for total cash of the register for a shift, you put $842.00. You even wrote down

$842.00 instead of $482.00. You didn't double check the register receipt."

"If you have any more questions just give me a call, I'm heading out to lunch with Terrance. I'll be near the area just in case. Oh and by the way, Wendy's sounds great for lunch on Monday."

"I hate it when you're right." He says.

"I'm not right, you were just wrong. Just make sure you're not wrong next time."

Before I start to drive away I ask Terrance if he has a place where he wants to go to eat. I'm not picky, I eat just about everything.

"There's a restaurant in Mattapan called Flames that I haven't been to in a few years. It's a Jamaican restaurant and they have great food."

I never tried Jamaican food, but I am willing to give it a shot. I hate to drive in Mattapan; it is the worst part of Boston.

We arrive at the restaurant and there are pictures everywhere; most of them I can't even figure out what they are. From what I understand, I ordered something that has pig in it with green rice. I'm not sure what I ordered but it looks quite exotic and different. As skeptical as I am, I give it a shot. Terrance orders beef with orange rice and a soup-like substance. He clearly has a better idea of the food he is ordering, I on the other hand feel as though I am going in blind.

"Can we take our food to go? We'll go back to my place and eat it there."

"It's fine by me."

The restaurant didn't have many seats and I didn't want to eat it in my car. It only made sense to head back to his house to eat.

We eat our lunch and he turns to me and says, "I'm tired. I'm going to take a nap and after that we can go to the movies. Can you wake me up in an hour?"

"Ok, not a problem."

After thirty minutes, I too am feeling tired. I didn't want to bother him to tell him I was leaving; I just left without him knowing.

Later that evening at nine, Terrance calls me.

"How come you didn't wake me up?"

"I was tired as well and I didn't want to bother you.

He gets agitated and in a mild temper he responds, "I wanted you to wake me up. I wanted you to come in my room and wake me up."

I didn't understand what the big deal was. He was upset that I didn't go into his room and wake him up from his nap? Something didn't make sense to me.

"I have work early in the morning. I couldn't stay too long regardless."

"Fine," he says, "We'll hang out some other time."

"Yeah that's fine, we can do that."

I hang up the phone and I'm still confused as to why he would be so agitated that I didn't wake him up. Something didn't seem right about him, about that moment. But truthfully, nothing seemed sane about him. He was a very interesting individual. I guess we are all interesting.

CHAPTER THIRTY-EIGHT

With everything going so well, I wanted to follow my Professor's words of wisdom by planning a vacation. I planned a vacation to visit California. I had always wanted to visit San Francisco and Los Angeles. Coaching the Giants in Cambridge had made the San Francisco Giants my favorite team to root for outside of the Boston Red Sox. On the way back I will visit my mother, and my brother and his family in Texas. I have mapped out my trip to be nine days. I planned on spending five days in California and four days in Texas.

The day before I leave to go to California, a duplicate money order prints by accident for $300. When this happened before, I called Colin, who trained me months before. I remembered the conversation as if it was yesterday.

"Colin, I have a duplicate money order that has printed by accident, what do I do with it?"

"Frank, you can do one of two things. If you have the money, you can swap the money for the money order and put it in your name and deposit it in your bank. Or you can cash it at the bank and put it in with the daily amount."

The first two times this happened, it was for $55 and $100. I happened to have the money both times. This time, however, I didn't have the money in my wallet. I went to the bank to cash the money order. I decided to put it in my name and cash it at the bank and then put it in the money bag when I get back to the store.

I hand the teller the money order.

"Do you have an account with us?"

"I don't but Mancini's has an account."

"Yes, but the money order is in your name."

"Can't you just cash it? It's a money order."

"No we can't."

"What do you mean you can't cash it? That's what I was told to do."

"Since you don't have an account with us, we can't cash it because we don't know if the money order has been stolen or if it's still active. It takes three days for a money order to clear."

"I'll be back."

I leave disgusted that I followed directions by the training supervisor and he was wrong. I was not going to put it in my bank account, especially since I was going on vacation the next day. I had money aside for my trip; I wasn't going to intertwine any of my money with theirs.

I head back to the store. I'm not sure what I can do now.

"Aaron, I don't know what to do. I don't have the money because I don't know what to expect when I get to California. I don't have a lot of money but I have enough. I was going to put the money from the money order into the money bag but they won't let me cash it."

"Can you just put the money order in the safe until you get back?"

"I guess I can do that."

Since it's already in my name, I can't have Aaron cash it. I'll just leave it in the safe until I get back.

I went the cheap way out when I bought my airfare. I bought a flight with a connecting trip from Boston to Philadelphia, then Philadelphia to San Francisco. I saved $200 doing that.

As the plane prepares to land in Philadelphia, there's a torrential downpour. The rapid shaking of the plane, the quick ups and down of the plane is making me sick. Just an hour plane ride has turned into the worst plane ride experience I have ever encountered. I hated flying to begin with, there's no way after this trip I am ever going on a plane again. I rather drive to Texas the next time I visit.

I arrive in San Francisco close to midnight. I have to call a transportation company because I notice my hotel is thirty minutes from the airport. It cost me $80.00 for the ride. That wasn't part of my spending plan.

The next day I rode on the public transit in order to get to the closest rental car place. I really want to rent a Chevy Camaro for my trip but it is $180.00 a day. I couldn't afford that. That is my dream car. I end up renting a Toyota Prius for $37.00 a day.

I drive down to Los Angeles. It takes me eight hours with some traffic. It was great to see things in person that I've only ever seen on television, such as Hollywood Boulevard and all the stars on the walk of fame. It reminded me of Times Square in New York. I decide to head over to the Hollywood sign.

As I arrive at the Hollywood sign, there are tons of people taking pictures. I interrupt a lady who is walking her small dog.

"Excuse me, do you mind taking a picture of me, please?"

"I don't mind at all. Where are you from?"

"I'm from Boston."

"I've been to Boston a lot. They have great plastic surgeons there. I've gone to a few of them."

"Our hospitals are the best in the nation. I'm in the middle of getting reconstructive jaw surgery and I'm confident enough that I am in the right hands for this type of procedure."

"They've done a great job on my face in the past. You'll do fine. You are in great hands with the Boston hospitals."

We talked for twenty minutes. She was a nice lady and after walking away from the conversation, I realized she must've been a TV star of some kind, perhaps a reality star or a soap opera actress. Her knowledge of plastic surgeons in Boston led me to believe this. I was convinced she was famous in one way or another but I didn't ask nor did I care. She was just like any other human being I have come into contact with before. That was probably the way she wanted it to be.

I planned on spending two days in Los Angeles. The first night I decided to go to Dodger Stadium and get a ticket to see the Dodgers play the Braves. Two weeks ago a Giants fan was bashed to death by a Dodgers fan. I did not want to let anyone know I was a Giants fan, but I am a baseball fan. I would love to go to every baseball stadium in major league baseball. I would love to throw the first pitch at Fenway Park. It's just one of a few things that would satisfy my simple pleasures in life. I don't get excited about much, but throwing the first pitch at America's most beloved ball park would do the trick. I would love to meet Bill Belichick and Terry Francona; the best two coaches to ever coach in Boston. That would be one of the greatest moments of my life. That's my once in a lifetime dream. My realistic dream is to go to every baseball stadium before I die. I would really love to travel cross country to every baseball stadium and beat the Guinness Book of World Records of going to every baseball stadium to watch a game in the fastest time possible. I know I can beat it if given the opportunity.

The Dodgers won 4 – 2 in a great pitching duel between Ted Lilly and Tim Hudson. Dodger stadium is one stadium to knock off my list before I die. Tomorrow I plan on going to Malibu Beach to watch the sunset, relax, and meditate. I don't meditate at all, but something deep down is suggesting I should do it before I leave. It will conclude my two day trip that I have planned here in Los Angeles.

The next day I arrive at Malibu Beach. It's a crisp, cool 70 degree day with the wind blowing gently enough to watch the sunset without getting too cold for a couple of hours. I climb over rocks to get to an area away from the highway and all of the noise. It's just me, in the middle of the rocks, hanging my feet down and gazing into the sun; listening to the waves crash upon one another and the sounds of the seagulls conversing with one another. This is relaxing to me. These silent waves are my only company. They give me peace from the troublesome events that I have encountered in the last year and a half. Now it's time to shut my eyes and let go of all the things I've been through and see what happens from there.

As I open my eyes, I look at my watch and to my surprise nearly three hours have gone by. Somewhere along meditating my mind went nowhere else it had ever gone before. Within those three hours a phrase that I have created continues deep in my mind: "Erase the pain of yesterdays, continue strong for today, positive thinking for future ways." I kept telling myself those three lines over and over again. It was something to help me throughout my troublesome times.

I walk back to my car and on a whim I decide to go the long way back to San Francisco, Route 1 to US 101; the Coastal Highway. Route 5 on the way down was all green land, pretty boring but I heard the Coastal Highway was an exciting route to take. It will take longer to get back, but I would love to see what everyone was talking about.

As I'm driving up the mountain side, I can feel the sudden sense of urgency as if I'm going up a roller-coaster ride getting ready for the exciting drop that occurs right after. I see signs to turn back because of a landslide that occurred a month ago, but I still want to go as far as I can; hopefully I don't have to turn around.

The exciting sensation of seeing how close I am to the edge is thrilling. I am absolutely afraid of heights, but this experience gives me chills up and down my spine. At any point a car can lose control and fall off the cliff. At every turn, I must approach it slowly to prevent a disastrous outcome. The fog is making the exciting twists and turns much harder to see the further I go up the mountain side. Some cars are parked at what seems to be a hiking trail. That is something I am going to do on another day. This is the most fun I've had driving, ever. So close to the edge, hundreds of feet before hitting the ground. As I make another bend, flashing yellow lights and an orange sign beam a message:

"ROAD IS CLOSED. TURN AROUND"

Nearly forty-five minutes have passed since I approached the mountain side and reached this road block. I have to turn around. Vastly disappointed I can't finish my travels on the U.S. Coastal Highway; I turn around and find another way back to San Francisco. This is something I want to finish at some point. I've never felt such excitement traveling by car.

After my two days back at San Francisco going on the Cable Cars, visiting and taking pictures at the Golden Gate Bridge, Oakland Coliseum, Candlestick Park, AT&T Park, and The Fisherman's Wharf, it's time to head to Texas and see my family.

I only spent four days in Texas but after only the first day, I already want to go back to California. It was great to see my mother, my brother and his family, but as soon as I got there, it wasn't the same. I had five days of not hearing anyone. No phone calls, no texts, absolute quietness from everyone. On my own with no one complaining, not one word about anything negative about me or anyone else. It was something I needed.

I'm getting to the point that I don't want to hear anyone complain about anything. I've been through a lot and barely told a soul about it. I just wish someone could be in my shoes and see how they would've handled things. The littlest things people complain about is nothing compared to what I've gone through. How I've pulled through it is astonishing to some people. I haven't lost control nor would I ever think I would. I broke down emotionally; that's the closest I will ever bend before breaking.

It's time to head back home and let reality give me all it's got. I'm mentally ready for anything. I enjoyed the time away; it was quite relaxing in California. I bought each coach on my staff a San Francisco Giants key chain that flashes their name. I bought a dozen key chains and magnets from Los Angeles and San Francisco. I'll let everyone decide which one they want at the afterschool program on a first come first serve basis.

I'm coming back with a different perspective on life. I'm not going to let Ashley bring me down anymore. He might've gotten away with what he did to me, but he won't get the best of me. I'm stronger than he thinks I am. I just wish the perception would go away. I know it won't, so I just have to prove to people that I'm not what the flyer depicts. Adam's jokes have been going on long enough. The only way I can put a stop to it, is to take a chance and stand up to him once and for all.

CHAPTER THIRTY-NINE

I still have a couple of more days off before going back to work, but I still have baseball practice. At the beginning of the practice I hand all my coaches their key chains and they are thankful for the gifts. At the end of our practice I am confident that this team, barring any injuries, can compete to be one of the top teams this year. We may actually be a contender for this year's Mayor's Cup.

For now, I must do my best to prepare my team to compete for the Mayor's Cup. We have won the playoffs the past two years. We have done extremely well since I've been able to draft the players on this team. Now if only we could be the best team in the division for the Mayor's Cup; that in itself will be a victory.

As practice is concluding, I see Adam drop by the field with his son from a Babe Ruth game.

"Excuse me Adam, can I talk to you."

"Sure Bud, what's going on?"

"Adam, could you please not joke about the flyer mentioning little kids around me? It really bothers me ever since the flyers first circulated. I understand you may think it's a joke, but to be honest, it bothers me deeply."

"Sure Frank, I didn't know it was bothersome and I will stop as long as you want me to."

I didn't know if he was going to stop or not. I would just have to wait and see what would happen.

"Thanks Adam."

After twelve days off from work I'm finally back at the grind. I arrive nice and early at six o'clock on a Wednesday morning. As I walk in, Terrance is shocked to see me so early. He scampers back into the store from smoking a cigarette.

"Terrance, did I catch you off guard?"

"You're never in this early."

"I am sometimes but I thought I'd get a head start with work this morning. I want to check the past week and a half of shortages/overages to see if there were any mistakes. I'm just making sure everything is as good as I left it.

"Frank, when are we going to hang out again?"

"I'm not sure Terrance, let me see how the rest of the week goes and I'll let you know. I'm sure I have some catching up to do."

"Just let me know, when you can. You're my only friend."

Aaron comes walking in to relieve Terrance from his duties.

"How was your vacation?"

"I had a great time. It was the best vacation I have ever taken, and I was by myself which made it even better. Some alone time was the best thing for me."

"I don't know how anyone can enjoy a vacation by themselves. You have no one to share the good times with."

"No you don't, but at the same time, you don't have anyone who will prevent you from doing anything you want. You get to do whatever you want, however you want, without anyone saying no or that they are too tired."

"I didn't think of it that way. Sounds like you had a great time by yourself."

"I learned a few things while I was in California."

"You didn't have a near-death experience and find God did you?"

"I would say it felt like I had a near-death experience. I drove on a road that was at an edge of a mountain side and if there was one small jerk of the wheel, I could've plummeted to my death."

"On the mountain cliff side, I felt how close I could be to death and that made me realize a few things. You just never know how quickly your life could change."

"But no, I didn't find God. C'mon you know me better than that. I don't believe in God. If people have a hard time trusting people, how can they trust someone who never shows his face? I know I'm stronger without believing in God. I don't need someone trying to weigh me down on something that's not real."

Thursday morning Aaron opens the bottom safe to make change and then comes into my office.

"Frank, don't forget about this money order that you left here when you went on vacation.

"That's right Aaron. Thanks for reminding me."

I head over to my bank that I barely use. I just have a few bucks in it with no debit card. I deposit the money order into my account because that's what I was told by my training manager. I just have to wait until it clears so I can put it back into the safe. I can't even replace the money with my own cash because I don't have any money left. After coming back from vacation, I am completely wiped out of cash from the great time I had in California. It was definitely worth it. It will take two to three days to confirm that the money order wasn't stolen or cashed. Once it clears, I will put it back into the safe Monday or Tuesday morning.

CHAPTER FORTY

Monday morning comes rolling around and as I walk into my store, Burt, the lost prevention supervisor is here.

"Good morning Frank, this is Leo. I'm training him for lost prevention and we are just doing an audit so he knows how to do it."

I reply, "There is a $300.00 shortage because I'm waiting for a money order to clear to replace a duplicate money order that printed by accident right before I went on vacation."

"Why didn't you just put Mancini's name on the money order and put it in with the daily cash?"

"I was never told to do that. When I called Colin at the time it happened, he told me a few ways in which I could fix it, but that was not one of them. He told me that if I have money on me, I can replace it and put the money order in my account after, or I can cash the money order at a bank and put in the bag afterwards. The first two times this happened I had the money on me; those were small amounts, $55.00 and $100.00."

"This time, I didn't have the money because it was $300.00 so signed it and tried to cash it. They said I couldn't cash the money order; that I need an account to cash it and it would take two to three days to clear."

"It's a money order! It doesn't need time to clear! That's bullshit."

"Listen, I did exactly what I was told to do."

Burt calls Miranda and tells her about the situation. She stops what she is doing and makes her way to my store.

"Do you have the money?"

"Yes, it should've cleared by now."

"Ok, go get it."

I head over to the bank; it shows that the money order has cleared. I took out the $300.00, which I was going to do today anyway and brought it back with me.

I hand it to Burt.

"Here count it. Make sure it's all there. I don't want you accusing me of putting it back without someone counting it, and when you count the safe after that it will not be shorter than you thought."

"Don't talk back to me."

"Don't assume I'm stealing. Because that's what your behavior suggests right now. I told you the truth and it is funny how you think I'm lying. Ask Aaron, he'll tell you exactly how it happened."

Miranda comes storming into the store and asks, "Why would you do something like that?"

"I didn't do it on purpose. I called Colin when it first happened months ago. This is the third time this happened. The only difference is that I didn't have the money to replace it and I tried to cash it at the bank, but they told me it takes a couple of days to clear because they have to make sure it's not stolen or already cashed."

"That's absurd. It's a money order, it's just like cash."

"No, Miranda. That isn't what the bank told me."

"It doesn't matter. You're suspended pending an investigation."

"I can't believe this. I did exactly what I was told and now you're suspending me because I listened to Colin. Whatever happened to me being trained as a manager? I still have yet to complete this training course you promised me over a year ago. You tossed me into a position without proper training and whenever I had a question, I would call Colin and even though I followed protocol according to what was said, you have the audacity to say I was wrong. Is there anyone in this company that doesn't contradict themselves? I've never done anything wrong up to this point and when I tell the truth you think it's a lie. I might as well start lying; it might make more sense to you."

"Get out of here, we'll give you a call sometime this week."

"This is bullshit. Do you want me to think what I did was wrong and write a one-page story of why I'm sorry? Oh wait, you don't care. Why don't you think about what I've done for the company and weigh out the options. That might actually seem like common sense so you probably don't know how to comprehend that."

Clearly I'm upset of the accusations Miranda and Burt are implying. I've never been suspended before in my life and I'm always putting sixty hours of work in when I'm scheduled to work fifty. But they don't see that. They only see what they want to see, not the truth.

A couple of days later I receive a call from the Human Resource manager and he asks me to have a meeting with him at my store with the Regional Manager on Thursday. Once HR gets involved in anything with any company, anyone in their right mind would know it's a sign of dismissal.

With this in mind, I still accepted to talk with them. Thursday comes along and the Regional Manager calls me.

"Frank, are you at the store?"

"That's what you asked me to do…right?"

"Yes, we are running late, we'll be there soon."

"Ok, I'll be right here waiting."

I'm pacing back and forth thinking of situations that could arise and certain smart ass comments that might come out of my mouth. Once I find out where this conversation is heading, I'll know what to say. I go inside the store and see Sean at the counter.

"Today's the day my friend. I doubt they're keeping me. Even though I told the truth, they are going to let me go.

"Don't say that, you didn't do anything wrong."

"Not in their eyes. I can tell."

The HR Manager and the Regional Manager walk in the door. The HR Manager is holding a folder. I know by observing people in the past on what this means. We walk into the back of the store where we can talk.

"So Frank, tell us your story."

"I don't have a story. You've already heard from Miranda and everyone else. Why should I repeat myself when you've already made up your mind on what to do with me?"

"What are you talking about?"

"Obviously that folder represents my dismissal. I'm not stupid by any means. You can cut all the small talk out and just come out and say it."

"Well Frank, you're right."

"Yeah I was right with the money order situation too. But you only want to believe what you want to believe."

"You don't have to be a jerk about it."

"It's funny how I'm being the jerk when I'm defending myself when I told the truth."

"We can't let you continue to work here if anyone else finds out what you did."

"What I did? I did what I was told. Did you look into the fact that I wasn't trained as a manager yet? That I've been neglected for fourteen months since I've been hired as an assistant manager in which I was promised to be properly trained and I never was. Next time make sure your management team follows through on what they say. People hate it when everyone is honest. I bet you hate me right now for being honest."

"It's best we cut ties."

"Like I expect you to keep me now considering I'm being truthful. Tell me something that will surprise me."

They didn't expect me to be so frank with them. That's how I am. Especially when I know they are wrong. I come out with everything and anything I remember that will flabbergast their thought process. I make people know what they did wrong, especially when I know I am right.

I'm walking out of the store, shrugging my shoulders to Sean as if to say, 'this is it'. Just two weeks coming back from a cleansing vacation, I had lost my job. If I didn't go on vacation, this would've never happened. Everything happens for a reason. Or at least, that is what I told myself.

CHAPTER FORTY-ONE

It's Monday morning and this is the first week in about a year that I won't be working over sixty hours. I can tell that it is going to be a long day.

Memorial Day weekend is coming up, and since I only work at the after school program, I have a little more free time. Today's weather is pretty miserable. It's raw with rain off and on. I'm taking my usual day off morning visit to Verna's Donut shop. I've never tasted a better donut that's so sweet, plus the donut is enormous for such a cheap price. I'm enjoying the day and reading the Boston Herald. I always start by reading the sports section first and then work my way to the front of the paper. The sports section is the most important section; I don't care about the news. Knowing about my sports first thing in the morning is more important than any news I may glance at after. As I am reading the paper, I receive a phone call from my former co-worker, Terrance.

For two months he's been asking me to hang out with him again. He's playing the card that he has no other friends and he says that I'm the closest thing he has to a friend. Although our last encounter was very strange, I always give people a second chance; that's just who I am. Knowing I have most of the day off and nothing else going on until work at two. I decide to go over his house for a few hours.

I arrive at his house slightly after 10:30am. He opens the door and says, "You're here a little earlier than I expected. Just go take a seat in the living room; I have to take a quick shower."

As I walk into his house, there is an awful stench in the air. It is a combination of cigarettes, marijuana, and whatever other drugs he may have been using with the combination of dirty laundry; the smell is unbearable. I have to open a window in the living room just so I can breathe. As I am waiting, I turn on the TV.

After he comes out of the shower, he says to me, "I have something for you to see."

We walk over to the kitchen where there is a hand-painted portrait.

"I know you're into psychology. I want you to look at this and tell me what you see. I want to know what you think of it."

"I'll give it my best analysis."

As I am carefully looking at this large portrait, I point out the first thing that comes to my mind.

"These dark colors in the middle of the portrait where this evil character is smiling, this tells me that this person is not mentally stable. This person can be very violent when someone gets him upset."

"Interesting, go on."

"Can I ask you a question pertaining to this?"

"Yes of course, go ahead."

"How long ago did you paint this?"

"How do you know I painted this?"

"You left your journal behind one night and this painting reminds me quite vividly of your style of writing. It's obvious to me that you committed a crime some time ago. If you don't mind me asking, what was it?"

"What do you mean?"

"The blood is oozing out of the person over here and that evil smile being very close to the person indicates to me that you enjoy watching someone suffer."

"I'm not going to tell you what crime I committed but I am quite surprised with your observation."

His voice is starting to escalate. He is clearly offended by the truth I revealed.

He quickly changes the subject. "Hey, let's go rob a bank."

"What? Are you serious?"

"Yes, I'm serious."

First of all, I'll never rob a bank and secondly, you will never do it because you will get caught."

"I'll get caught?"

"Yes Terrance you'll get caught. You will get caught because even though you're a smart guy, you don't have enough common sense. You are the type of person that could plan it but not keep in mind the little things that will leave evidence behind. You will think that everything was done right but you will screw up somewhere. You won't be able to do it, because everyone gets caught and you are no exception."

He does not take this lightly. After the words that I say, he goes to his room and within seconds he comes up behind me and puts his left arm around my throat.

"I never wanted to do this but I have to."

At first, I think he is just playing around; but as I look over to the right, I notice a knife and suddenly I am petrified. The knife has a four inch blade with a green handle. I'm looking frantically at the knife trying to keep an eye on it and trying to listen to what Terrance is saying. Focusing on the knife, knowing that my life is at stake, I try to focus my attention towards his demands.

"You nailed it right on the head, I did commit a crime a few years back and I did some time for it. But enough about me, I know what you did last year and you got away with it!"

"What you are talking about?"

He drags me into his room and takes out the flyer that was posted all over the City of Cambridge.

"How did you get this?"

"I took it from your glove compartment when we went to lunch that day. I knew you did something wrong and I tried to look for evidence online but I couldn't find it so now I have to handle the situation myself."

"What are you talking about, I never did anything!"

Terrance then screams, "THIS IS WHAT I'M TALKING ABOUT. DON'T PLAY STUPID, YOU MOLESTED CHILDREN AND YOU GOT AWAY WITH IT."

"No I didn't, someone made it up."

I try to explain myself, but every time I do, the situation keeps getting worse. I start to sweat profusely, scared of what Terrance is capable of doing. Knowing now that he is capable of horrific crimes, I can only imagine what he may do.

"DO NOT FUCKING LIE TO ME, NO ONE WOULD MAKE UP SOMETHING LIKE THIS. YOU GOT AWAY WITH IT BUT NOW I HAVE TO DO SOMETHING ABOUT IT."

At that point, I am completely quiet. I don't want to say anything else because it seems that every time I try and defend myself, his temper and aggressive manner only becomes worse. As I'm sitting on the floor, shaking and sweating, I'm trying to figure out how to get away.

"Don't you dare think of running out of here, I will use this knife. You don't want to rob a bank with me so I will rob you."

He grabs me by the neck, demanding I take out my wallet. With little air left to breathe, I grab my wallet and open it right in front of him. My wallet is completely empty. In disgust, he pushes me towards the ground and without hesitation, grabs my arm, picks me back up and holds tightly to my jacket and drags me towards my car.

Conveniently for him, he lives on a dead end street and his house is the last one on the street. We are not in public view as he lives right in front of the East Boston Marsh. I could not receive help from anyone.

"Get into the passenger seat and work your way over to the driver's seat. I'm not letting go so don't try to do anything stupid."

As we get in the car he yells at me, "Give me your phone and drive to the nearest ATM and don't try and do anything stupid, I will use this knife."

After a few minutes, Terrance barks, "WHERE ARE YOU GOING!"

With sweat pouring off of me like Niagara Falls, I reply to him in a trembling voice, "I'm going to the nearest ATM I know, which is the Bank of America at Bell Circle."

"I don't know this area, don't fuck with me. Get to a bank as soon as possible."

"It is right over here." I'm pointing towards the rotary in front of us.

As we are pulling in the parking lot he vehemently says to go through the drive thru ATM.

"I want you to take out $1,000."

"I don't have $1,000."

"Listen," he says with his face right in front of mine holding the knife to my left, "I know you have money, you just got back from California and you always say how you are on a great savings plan. DON'T FUCK WITH ME. THIS IS THE LAST TIME I'M GOING TO ASK TWICE ABOUT ANYTHING OR YOU WILL REGRET IT."

Again, the lack of common sense is evident. Usually when someone goes on vacation, they use money. I was on a great savings plan to take a trip to California. He is clearly on top of the no common sense chain.

I try to take out a $1,000 and the ATM says:

ABOVE DAILY LIMIT.

Terrance reads the receipt. He looks at me and says, "Take out $500.00."

It was able to process that transaction. Then he says, "Take out your other card and take out another $500.00."

"I don't have another card to use."

"I want you to use that card and go into your savings account and take out $500.00 from there and then I want the receipt."

The knife is up against the right side of my neck, where it would be out of sight of the camera. As the transaction is finishing up, he says, "Now I want you to drive to the Tobin Bridge."

On our way towards the Tobin Bridge, he's trying to go through my phone.

"Put in your fucking password! I know you're hiding pictures of little kids on your phone and I'm going to find them!"

Knowing I have nothing to hide, I unlock my phone.

"Where are your pictures and videos?"

Like I said before, his common sense is lacking. There are icons that are specifically labeled 'videos' and 'gallery'. I didn't have any videos on it; I very rarely even take pictures on my phone. The only two pictures on my phone were of my nephew, who was born six months ago.

"Where are your other pictures?"

"What are you talking about? I don't have any other pictures."

"I know you have pictures of little kids here and I will find them."

He never found anything and I tried telling him that but he was too stubborn. He didn't want me to speak another word. He was aggravated that he couldn't find anything.

"I want you to go back to a bank and take out $462.00."

At first I thought to myself, $462.00 is such an odd amount. Why would he want $462.00? To me, it seemed like he got himself in debt from a drug situation. Considering he has confided in me in the past that he smokes weed, has taken ecstasy, used cocaine and many others, he could be in trouble with drugs.

I move suddenly in the vicinity of my phone and Terrance thinks I am trying to defend myself. He says, "Don't even think about moving again. You are lucky the knife is in the other hand."

He then moves the knife from his right hand to his left hand where it would be closer to me.

"Drive to the Maverick Square bank and take out more money."

"As I stated before, I don't have any more money."

"Do whatever it takes so you can to take out the money because I need that money. If you don't get it to me, I am going to keep your phone. It is going to be $462.00 or your phone."

I park the car and take the keys out of the ignition. As I am leaving the car, Terrance decides to come in with me. He follows me to make sure I won't run away. This ATM is a walk-in ATM. I am waiting in line; there is one older gentleman in front of me and Terrance is waiting in the back for the gentleman to leave. As the guy turns around, he asks me a question, "Are you ok kid?"

My skin must be beet red, because I can feel the beads of sweat rushing down my face. I stutter as I reply, "Yes, yes I'm ok."

The gentleman leaves without any other questions.

I try to withdraw more money out, but the ATM says OVER DAILY LIMIT. I print out the receipt and show it to Terrance. I have my head down and shrug because I have no idea what else he wants me to do.

As we are walking back to the car, I'm completely quiet because I don't know what's going to happen next. With my hands shaking, I'm trying to put the key into the ignition and I drop my keys on the floor. I quickly look over to the right and I see a devilish smile as he continues to look around in my phone. To me this is clearly a sign of a mentally unstable individual. I start the car, turn to him and ask, "Where are we going now?"

"Just drive until I tell you where to go."

I must have been driving for at least an hour all around Chelsea and East Boston before he finally says something.

"I want you to park over here."

I turn right onto a one way street and then he points to the left and says to park in front of the church.

"I am going to give you your phone back, but I am going to erase everything on it. All your games, pictures, videos, and whatever you may have hidden will be deleted. Write down all the numbers you have in your phone and after that, I will erase everything and give you your phone back."

I write down thirty-three numbers; most of them are coaches and parents from the league. After I am done writing the numbers, I put the piece of paper down to grab my phone. Terrance then swipes the list of numbers and keeps them. I have no idea why he wants the numbers but I wasn't going to say anything. He gives me my phone back, which must have meant my days ahead were looking better.

"I want you to drop me off at Dunkin Donuts in Chelsea."

I start the car back up, still confused as to why he wanted the phone numbers and start heading towards the Dunkin Donuts on Broadway.

"I want you to park right next to this car, right before the Dunkin Donuts."

I pull over, double parked as he requested. I put the car in park and he leans over to me and says, "I never want to see your fucking face again, you disgust me. Once I leave this car, I never want to hear your name or see you anywhere. Do not go to the police or I will kill you. Do not tell Aaron either. I don't want him to speak of you at all. If I hear your name just once, I will go to the police and say you molested my nephew and after I show them the flyer, they'll believe me. Do you understand that?"

"Yes." I reply. I am in a frightened state of shock with the blade of the knife only millimeters away from my face.

After Terrance retrieved one of these flyers, he insisted that I did something but he didn't understand that none of it was true. There were never any accusations, the police investigated the matter and found that there were no allegations relevant to the flyers. Terrance never believed me; I would've been arrested or on the news if any of it was true.

Blind perception takes over the mind and when it does it can never be erased no matter how innocent a person is. I was yet again blamed for something I never did because of Ashley, who had nothing better to do than to try and ruin a man's reputation.

After Terrance left my car, I drove away instantly. I had no idea where I was going; I just wanted to get away. I drove for about an hour and parked the car at the baseball field behind the school where I work.

I sat in my car.

I put the seat all the way back and just laid there.

I had no idea how much time had gone by. All I remember is that I just wanted it to be over, and considering what I'd gone through and what Terrance had said to me, I felt that it is now over.

I went into Kim's office and asked for the day off; an hour before I'm supposed to start.

"Is everything ok Frank? You never ask for a day off."

"Something came up, I need to go."

"Ok, go ahead. Let me know if you need anything."

Kim granted me the day off without any knowledge of what was going on.

I went home.

I lock my bedroom door and I lie on my bed for a few hours until I am able to gather myself together.

A few hours later and I decide to call Damien, to tell him what had happened earlier in the day.

"Damien, a few hours ago I was held up because of the flyer from two years ago. He has the phone numbers of the parents and coaches from the league. I am telling you what happened because if Terrance calls those numbers for any reason, I need to know. Right now, it is just hearsay and it will be hard to prove from the cameras that he held me up."

"Frank, I'm going to call Sam and see what he has to say."

Considering the lack of support from Sam a year ago, I didn't anticipate him doing much regarding this matter. He was just a typical lawyer, looking for money before deciding to get involved with anything.

He fits the well-known stereotypical reputation of a Jew. I have many Jewish friends, none of which were as pathetic as Sam. If any of my other friends were lawyers, I knew they would be there to help me. Sam was no friend of mine. If Sam wasn't Jewish, he probably would be supporting me through it all, and we would be able to get the culprit who started this to begin with. Sam was a typical cheap person. I needed him to try and put money aside for a change, but yet all he saw were the dollar signs.

When something horrible happens to me, I usually do one thing; I quietly move along without recourse. I believe in karma, what goes around comes around. I've always helped my friends through their situations. Sam may have cared less about me, but that was fine because I became used to it. I knew that Terrance would make a mistake and once he did, he would pay for what he had done to me. He had a reputation of having a big mouth and even if I had gone to the police at that point, it would have just been considered hearsay. There may have been video evidence of Terrance showing him next to me at the two ATM's. However, it would be difficult to see the knife in the surveillance. I needed him to tell at least two people. Once he opened his mouth to more than one person, then I could get him arrested. I just had to patiently wait for him to slip up.

During Memorial Day weekend, My Aunt Tracy asked for my help with her shop. Memorial Day Weekend was the biggest weekend for her. As I got there early Sunday morning, just six days after Terrance held me up, he tried calling me. I recognized his number, I didn't pick it up. Within seconds of declining his call, I received a text message:

"I know ur there, and if you don't call me now then imma fuck up your shit."

I didn't respond to his message. At that point I called Sam. Although it was early Sunday morning, he told me to call him if anything else happened and I did just that. I told him what Terrance had said; Sam said he would call me right back.

Sam never called me back.

The next day, I see Aaron calling me. He never calls me, he usually texts me; but I was thinking he needs help with work and although I don't work there anymore, I could still help him figure out some problems. I answer the phone and after saying hello, I hear Terrance's voice.

I hang up right away.

Aaron doesn't know what Terrance had done to me. He let Terrance borrow his phone without knowing that Terrance would be harassing me.

With Terrance using Aaron's phone, I wasn't sure if he would try using anyone else's. With that idea in my head, I became weary of any blocked calls or unknown numbers. I couldn't let Terrance get any more pleasure of harassing me that way.

CHAPTER FORTY-TWO

As a team, we are off to our best start since I have taken over the Giants five years ago. We are in first place and at this time in late May, we have a two game lead for the division title. Even during our push to the Mayor's Cup, I am able to hide my depression, although it has gotten worse since I lost my job at Mancini's, and being held up at knifepoint by Terrance; I'm trying to the best of my ability to run this team the best way I can in such a time of dismay.

With just four weeks left to go in the baseball season and having a two game lead on everyone else, I attend every major game I can, to root for the team that's lower in the standings to win. This would make it harder for teams to catch up to us.

Today's game is the Astros against the Nationals. As the two teams are practicing, a batter hits a hard foul ball into the stands.

Someone drops quickly to the ground.

I run over to the person who has just been hit with the foul ball.

It's Larry's wife.

I shout out, "Larry, your wife was just hit with the ball. Come over here quick!" She groans in pain. Her head is swelling, with blood dripping down her ear.

"Someone call 9-1-1. Everybody back up. Somebody grab an ice pack. She's been hit in the head."

After I give Larry the ice pack, he starts to take control of his wife. I back up a few steps, I turn around and I see Justin. Justin comes to see what's going on from down the field. He notices that it's his mother who is seriously hurt.

He starts crying.

He's worried about his mother. I can't bear to watch him in the emotional state that he's in. I begin to shed a few tears as well. I don't like to see anyone hurt, but if they are, I make sure I am the first one there to help them out, no matter who they are.

As the ambulance arrives, Larry's wife is being sent to the nearest hospital. Before Larry jumps into the back of the ambulance he shouts over to me, "Frank, make sure my son is alright and I'll call you with what's going on. Thanks for helping us."

"I will."

As they leave to go to the hospital, I turn to Justin, "Justin, your mother is going to be ok. I know how overwhelmed you are right now. I was in the same position with my mother a few years ago. She wasn't alright at first but everything turned out ok. I'll be here if you want to go to the hospital and see her, but we have to

270

wait for your father to call. For now, just hang out with your friends and I'll come down to get you once I hear anything."

"Ok, Frank. I'll be down there." He points to the swing set area.

"Yeah that's fine. Go and try to get your mind off of what just happened. Do you need anything?"

"Can I get a drink?"

"Yeah sure, here's two dollars. Go get whatever you want."

Justin is fourteen. He can take care of himself. But in a moment like this, I just want to make sure that someone is here for him if he needs anyone to talk to. I mentored him for a few years and I am good friends with his family. He looks up to me as a big brother which he has said to his friends in the past.

An hour goes by and Larry calls me.

"Frank, my wife is seriously hurt. Can you drop Justin off at the hospital? She's going to be transferred to another hospital, but she wants to make sure she sees Justin before we go there. After that, would you mind picking up my daughters down the street and then head to the Boston hospital? Oh and another thing, please don't tell anyone how seriously hurt my wife is. We don't want the kid who hit her to get upset."

"Not a problem Larry, I can do that. We'll be there soon."

I hang up the phone and rush over to get Justin.

"C'mon Justin lets go. I have to drop you off at the hospital."

"Is everything ok?" He asks worriedly.

"As good as it can be right now."

I'm trying to hide the fact that she's not doing that great.

"I have to pick up your sisters after I drop you off."

I make it to the hospital in five minutes. Larry is waiting out in front of the ambulance for Justin. Justin hops out of the car and heads into the ambulance with his mother and father.

"Frank, my daughters are in the community center right down the street. You know where it is right?"

"Yeah, yeah go. I know where I'm going." I reassure him.

I make it to the community center in minutes. "C'mon girls lets go. Do you know what happened?"

"No, we just know our mother was hurt."

"Yes she was. I'm taking you to the hospital now."

They have no idea how seriously hurt their mother is. To be completely honest neither do I. I just know it is bad enough that they have to send her to a Boston hospital.

We arrive at the hospital in twenty-five minutes. The girls go to their brother and I head right over to Larry.

"How serious is it?"

"She has a skeletal fracture, internal bleeding in the ear, and a shot ear drum. She's going to be fine as long as the bleeding stops. They have to take more x-rays throughout the night and tomorrow to see if there's a difference after the swelling goes down. She's conscious, they are running a few tests now and we'll be able to go in soon, but they will only allow two people in the room at a time."

"It sounds like pretty good news since the first time you called me."

"It is definitely better than when I first called you. I didn't know how severe it was at that point."

We wait an hour and the nurse finally comes out.

She walks towards Larry.

"Everything seems to be coming out ok. We still have to monitor her for a few days to make sure nothing gets worse. But at this point, everything is looking good."

"Can we see her?"

"Yes you can. But only two people at a time."

I chime in. "Can her three kids go together? I know you said only two but you can't leave one of them out."

"Yes, that's fine. All three of them can go in."

The nurse directs the three of them to see their mother first.

"How are you doing Larry?"

"I'm hanging in there. I'm better than I was before. But it's still shocking to me."

"It's going to be. She's your wife and you love her to death. I can only imagine how you feel right now. But it seems like the worst is behind you now. Everything is progressing the right way."

"Yeah it is and I can't thank you enough for what you've done for us."

"Larry, it's just the kind of person I am. No matter who it is, I would've done it the same way over and over again. I care about everybody."

I receive a phone call from Damien.

"Hello, Frank. How is she doing?"

"Hold on one second Damien."

I put my hand over the phone so that Damien doesn't hear me.

I turn to Larry, "Larry, Damien is on the phone. Do you want to talk to him?"

"Yeah, I'll talk to him."

I get back on the phone with Damien.

"Larry's here, it would be best if you talk to him."

Larry tells Damien how his wife is doing.

They talk for no more than five minutes.

"Here Frank." He hands me my phone back.

"I didn't want to say anything to Damien because I didn't know what you wanted me to say about the incident." I explain.

"I know, I understand. Thanks."

His three kids come out. They seem to be doing ok. But I can tell they are in shock.

I walk in with Larry to see his wife.

"Hey there honey, how you doing?"

"I'm in pain but overall I could be worse, right?"

We start laughing then she starts laughing.

"Oww Oww. Don't make me laugh it hurts."

"You did it to yourself."

She looks up to me, "Frank, I just want to say thank you. You're a great person and although you and I haven't seen eye to eye on some occasions, I still want to say I appreciate what you've done for us."

"Wow, that ball must have really hit you hard."

She laughs again then grimaces in pain. "Take a compliment when you hear one."

"I'm sorry. It was just an opportunistic time to say it."

I'm friendly with everyone. There are times when Larry's wife can be a bitch but I don't let her get to me. Everyone can be a bitch from time to time. I've dealt with worse, if I can deal with Lisa, I can deal with anyone. Certain people and coaches have told me to watch out for Larry's wife's behavior but I didn't see anything wrong with it. She may be a bitch from time to time but that's normal from what I understand.

We spend twenty minutes in her room. As we head out the nurse asks Larry if he plans on staying with her. His wife interrupts.

"Larry, go home with the kids and pick up our car on the way. I'll be fine."

"Ok honey." He gives her a kiss. "I love you."

"I love you too."

We leave the room and meet the kids in the lobby.

"You guys ready?"

"Where's mom? Is she coming?"

"No she's going to be staying a couple of nights. They just want to make sure everything is ok. Frank will be driving us home tonight and we'll come back tomorrow. If you kids don't want to go to school, I understand."

Everyone gets into my car and I decide to put on JAM'N 94.5. It's the music they enjoy. I don't care too much for it. I'm going make the ride home as comfortable as I can. They start singing as certain songs come on.

At that point, I start talking to Larry.

"I heard you guys won tonight."

"We did?"

"Yes, you did. Jack sent me a text a little while ago."

Justin chimes in. "The Nationals are still better than the Giants. When are you coming to one of my Babe Ruth games?"

"I'll go to one sometime next week. I promise you that."

I arrive at their house and drop the kids off first. Larry and I wait for the kids to get into the house and then we head over to the baseball field where his car is.

"Frank, I can't thank you enough for what you've done today. I truly appreciate it."

"Larry, don't worry about it. That's what friends are for. I'll be there for you guys whenever I can be. I'm always there for my friends."

I drop him off at his car.

"Larry if you need anything, don't hesitate to call me. I only work at the school now so I have some free time. What time are you going to the hospital tomorrow?"

"I'm going to drop the kids off at school, if they go, and then I'm heading right over to the hospital right after."

"If it's not a problem I'll give you a call and meet up with you sometime tomorrow."

"Yes, that's fine. Give me a call tomorrow."

Larry's wife stays in the hospital for a few days. I stop by every day to make sure Larry is doing alright. He seems to be doing better knowing the fact that his wife is getting better. Larry tells me that they're not sure if there will be any side effects from
276

the skeletal fracture at this point. They still have to monitor her progress every week. But overall, everything seems to be going good. Larry and his wife had a conversation about suing the league, but after talking with them, they decided not to.

As I promised Justin a week ago, I am able to attend his game later this afternoon. For the past few weeks he's been asking me to go and he knows about my promises. I very rarely make a promise but when I do, I keep it.

As I grab a bag of sunflower seeds from my car, I see Larry's wife in their car. She's watching the game. I stop by to see her first.

"How's everything going?"

"It's coming along. Every day is progress and that's always a good thing."

"How come you're not sitting on the bench with Larry?"

"Are you kidding me? I'm never going to get out of this vehicle during a baseball game or any game again."

Just as she says that, a foul ball is hit towards us. The crowd yells, "HEADS UP!"

Larry's wife ducks while she is in her car.

"You know the ball isn't going to hit you if you're in the vehicle."

"It's just a reflex. I'm always going to do it no matter what. It's just something else to make fun of me for."

"Thanks for that open invitation to make fun of you. I'll keep a mental note of that."

"It's not like you don't do it now."

"This is true. But now I have more of a reason to do it. I'm going to go sit down with Larry."

"Go right ahead. I'll be reading my book."

As I make my way towards the bench, I see Damien sitting next to Larry. His son is on the other team. I notice that we are at the opponents' bench. It is closer to the parking lot, it naturally makes sense.

As I sit down next to Damien, I look over to see who the opponent is. It just so happens to be Ben's team and I see Lisa in their dugout. It seems that her boyfriend, Johnnie, Ben's coach, couldn't make it to today's game as he is nowhere to be found. I hadn't seen Lisa in almost two years and I hadn't talked to Ben since he warned me about Ashley; that was over two years ago.

Out of nowhere Justin runs over and steals my bag of sunflower seeds.

"Thanks Frank!" he exclaims as he runs back to the bench.

He doesn't know that I have another bag in my car. I don't need them that badly.

I'm talking to Damien and all of a sudden I hear Lisa yelling. I start tuning in on what she is saying. She's on the phone with someone.

"He's right next to the fucking bench. He doesn't have to be here. Why the fuck is he sitting right next to our bench? Can't you fucking do something about this? You're my fiancé, he's bothering both Ben and I. Do something!"

I turn to Damien. "Do you hear this?"

"What do you mean?"

"Listen to what Lisa is saying."

We both listen as Lisa is continuing to talk to who I think is Johnnie on the phone.

"This is fucking bullshit, can't you talk to him and tell him that he shouldn't be here."

Damien says to me, "Wow, she really is a bitch."

"I tried to tell you that."

"You're not doing anything wrong. You are here to watch a game. It's a free country. You can do whatever you like."

"Should I leave?"

"No. You have no reason to leave. You're not saying anything to her. And although I know you won't, I suggest that you don't."

"Of course I won't."

She continues her rant. But as she is doing so, I see Ben get up to the plate.

"Can't you fucking call the police and do something about this? He won't stop bothering us; he's literally fucking ten feet away. If you love me like you say you do, you'll do something about it!"

As Lisa is continuing her rant in a furious tone, I notice Ben's focus is directed towards what she is saying to her fiancé. I can tell it bothers him. He gets up to the plate and he swings at the first three pitches. All three pitches were way out of the strike zone. He doesn't want to be here. After he strikes out, he looks over to me and just from his subtle gestures I can tell he is sorry for his mother's rant. He understands the bitch she is and there is nothing he can do about it. Once he makes it back to the dugout, he viciously throws his helmet and bat in her vicinity. He is indirectly telling her to stop what she is doing but she is too stupid to pick up on it.

I stay for the entire game. Throughout the game Lisa continually talks to her fiancé, keeping him informed about my imaginary actions she is proclaiming that I'm doing. Even though she is lying to him over the phone, he doesn't know that. He believes everything that is coming out of her mouth.

I would leave but Damien insists I stay for the game. I have every right to be here like anyone else. There is no reason I should not be able to watch any game, let alone a game someone wanted me to attend.

Justin's team wins.

That win eliminates Ben's team from the playoffs. That's a moral victory in my book.

I hope that she won't cause a scene during Mayor's Cup weekend. She had caused a scene once before at my All-Star game two years ago. She is unpredictable, so I have no idea if she has anything else planned out in her mind. She is as crazy as they come.

CHAPTER FORTY-THREE

The day before the Mayor's Cup tournament I receive a text from Aaron:

U know how I was saying he officially lost his mind...well apparently Terrance bragged today about robbing you for $2,000.00...he's like a serial killer that wants to get caught. He was saying to tell you to drop the charges or you're gonna be in a world of trouble.

I don't respond to the text. I know that Terrance will make a mistake sooner or later. Terrance has finally bragged to somebody; he had only robbed me for $1,000 but felt the need to exaggerate. I need him to tell one more person and then I will go to the police.

My day has finally arrived. After all that I've been through, I take the Giants to the first game of the Mayor's Cup tournament. We won the division with an impressive 12 – 3 record. It is a complete 180 from last years' injury prone season of 3 – 13.

Dealing with so much the past year, this is my highlight. I've dealt with numerous unexplainable events in just the past few months. I really don't know how I survived mentally up to this point. These past few months I've been through hell, but I didn't break.

I don't let anyone in on my feelings. I seclude myself emotionally from everyone I come into contact with. They always think I'm cheerful but behind closed doors, I'm broken inside. Nobody needs to know that. I'm here in this world to make them happy and that's what I do each and every day. Being bullied in school has taught me many lessons and each time I have overcome those obstacles. This is the toughest battle of my life.

I prepare the Giants for the biggest game of their lives. I let the assistant coaches take over the majority of the pregame speech. This team strives on being the home team; it's been "good luck" in their eyes. We were 7 – 1 when we were the home team during the regular season.

During the coin toss, the opposing manager gives me permission to call it in the air.

"Tails."

The umpire bends down to pick it up.

"Tails it is. What do you decide?"

"We want to be the home team."

"Ok, we'll pick 3rd base side," the opposing manager adds.

We as a coaching staff appoint Eddie to pitch this game; he's been our ace all year.

In the first inning, Eddie struggles by having runners on first and second with no outs. The batter hits the ball towards our shortstop. As our shortstop picks up the ball, the runner going to 3rd runs into him. All the runners are safe.

I see the umpires coming together. I'm waiting to see what they have to say before I go out there. Before the umpires' break up the meeting, Andre's father pushes me towards them.

"Hold on. I'm seeing what they have to say first."

"Go out there now, you're the manager, you have the right to know what's going on."

I start making my way towards the umpire and they make a runner's interference call. The runner is out and it's back to runners on first and second with one out. The opposing manager is furious; he comes storming onto the field. After ten minutes of the manager arguing the call, he finally backs away and the game is continued where we left off. Eddie finishes the inning without giving up any runs.

The game starts to get out of hand in the 4th inning. We eventually lose the game 9 – 1, but I don't remember much more of it. My mind wasn't in it as much as I would've liked it to be. I didn't get to enjoy the game as I would have in years past. All the excitement I had in just wanting to get here is not there anymore. I had a lot on my mind and I couldn't seem to shake it. The past four months had been getting the best of me. The past two years had been troublesome. I just wasn't as happy as I used to be.

CHAPTER FORTY-FOUR

On July 4th, 2011, Larry's family invites me to go with them to see the fireworks behind the Museum of Science. I have nothing else going on, so why not?

I arrive at the Museum of Science and I am leaning up against a pillar. As I am looking into the Charles River, I hear a young lady say, "Such a beautiful view isn't it?"

I turn around to see if she is talking to me. She is right next to me and there isn't anyone else around. She's a short girl, about 5' 2"; a very petite brunette. She looks to be in her early twenties.

"Yes it is a great view. Are you here to see the fireworks too? I'm Frank and you are...?"

"I'm Rachel, nice to meet you."

"Do you come here often?"

"I come here every year. I live just a few blocks away."

We end up talking for the whole night. Once Larry's family arrives, I introduce Rachel to them. I didn't expect to meet anyone, but I guess no one really intends for that to happen, it just does.

She sits next to me during the fireworks. Rachel tells me that she has a four year-old daughter that she is able to see twice a week at a foster home. When she tells me this, a red flag pops up in my mind. It may be nothing, but now I become a little concerned. We make plans to grab a drink in Faneuil Hall after the fireworks.

As we talk in the bar, she asks me a series of questions,

"Are you serving in the military?"

"No, I am not."

"Did you serve in the military?"

"No, I did not."

"I thought you did. Your haircut represents a military style haircut."

"I'm sorry but I never served at all."

"Do you mind if I talk to someone else? Will you still be here?"

"No I don't mind, we aren't together. Do you want me to be here?"

"Yeah, I'll be right back."

After she says that, she approaches an African-American man dressed as a Marine.

I realize she was just looking for someone with a military background. There are so many reasons why she would do that but it's not my place to care. After finishing my beer, I walk out of the bar not acknowledging her. She isn't even aware that I left. As I thought about the red flags throughout the night, I knew I didn't want to deal with her at all. I had learned from my past experiences with Lisa to look out for certain signs before getting involved with somebody again.

Larry's family tells everyone about my date last night.

Everyone is asking about what happened and where I went. This is something I don't like; I don't like attention. I tell them that I hung out with her for the night, and that she has my number if she wants to call me. I don't tell them that I won't be hanging out with her again. It's none of their business anyway; they don't need to know about my personal life.

The next day, July 6th, a typical summer league game where most of the coaches scout the kids to be drafted this upcoming fall is taking place. I have to figure out who I want on my team for next year. Usually summer league games bring out the best in some players.

As I'm at the field, Mr. Baseball comes up to me.

"Hey Frank, did you go to the board meeting last night?"

"No, I had no idea that there was a meeting last night."

Mr. Baseball is just a coach; he's not part of the board but heard about it through another coach.

I start to walk towards Adam who is here to watch his daughters play.

"Adam, did you go to the board meeting last night?"

"Yes, I did. But I can't talk about it."

"What do you mean you can't talk about it?"

"I'm sorry Frank but it was a meeting about you. Just know that I defended you."

"You're saying that they had a meeting about me last night, talking about me?!"

"Yes but I really can't say anymore."

"Is there anything you can say Adam?"

"I told Sam and Damien that you babysat my three kids for a whole week, and that if I had any doubt about you as a person I wouldn't have even thought about asking you to babysit my children. But yet, we were standing there talking about you, without you there. First of all, I said you should be at the meeting to not only defend yourself but also chime in on what we don't know so you can elaborate on what happened to you and how it happened."

Now I'm starting to get irritated. There was a meeting held secretly about me. What could be so important that I was not aware of such a meeting?

I am going from coach to coach asking if there was anybody else at the meeting last night to try and figure out what else was said about me.

"Rodney did you go to the meeting last night?"

"Yes I did."

Finally, I find another coach who was at the meeting.

"Can you tell me what was said about me?"

"I'm not supposed to. But I can say it was a nasty meeting."

"Nasty? How?"

"Well, it was mentioned that you may be a pedophile."

"WHAT?!" I am furious at this point.

"Yes. The word pedophile was tossed around the room for almost the entire meeting. They are going to give you an ultimatum. They want you to either resign or go to the police and file a report on the man who held you up."

"They? Who are you referring to?"

"Sam and Damien; they said that you've caused an uprising. That Lisa was complaining that you were at her son's game."

"Damien was at the same game I was and I wasn't there for Ben. Damien was the one who told me that I shouldn't leave the game. I can't believe he's contradicting himself. Sam and Damien conducted the meeting?"

"Yes, but I didn't tell you that. I didn't say anything to you."

How could anyone say anything like that? I'd never done anything to any child. I'd never inappropriately put my hand on anyone. How could my own league slander me like that? No allegations, no accusations, but someone was still saying that I might be a pedophile behind my back. This is absolutely crazy.

I remember when I first went to Damien about the flyer two years ago and he told me, "Just ignore it and it will eventually go away."

I did that, I listened to what he had to say. I ignored it and now this is how they treat me! Here I am thinking that this league is like a family to me, and they go behind my back and talk about me.

I am pacing back and forth on the field and some of the few friends I have left in this league suggest that it may be best for me to walk away from here.

At this moment, I don't want to leave yet. I want answers and I want them immediately! I feel so empty inside. They might as well have torn my heart out, stomped it on the ground until it turned black and then stuffed it down my throat.

I want to call Damien right now. I walk away from the crowd so they don't hear what I have to say to him. I don't swear much, but when I do, it's because I'm in a lot of distress from what people have said or done to me that offends me. It takes a lot to offend me.

I call Damien.

I hear him pick up, but I don't give him a chance to say anything.

"Hey fuck you Damien."

"What's wrong?"

"You're asking me what's wrong. You son of a bitch! You had a secret meeting about me. Calling me names and you didn't have the audacity to include me in it. What the fuck is wrong with you?"

"Frank, just calm down and we'll talk about it soon. Don't worry about it."

"Don't worry about it! Fuck you! I can't believe you did something like this. You're an asshole!"

I hang up the phone and start to walk back to the field. As I am walking back, I run into Jack.

"Jack, did you go to the board meeting last night?"

"I didn't know we had a board meeting."

"Yes, there was a secret board meeting held last night about me. Calling me a pedophile and shit like that."

"I always check my email and I never received an email about a board meeting. Do you know why it was conducted?"

"It had to do with a person that held me up a couple of months ago, also, just last week I went to Justin's game and Lisa was there. She called her fiancé, saying that I was causing problems, but Damien insisted that I stay at the field."

"When did you get held up? How come you didn't tell me?"

"Honestly Jack, I never tell anyone what happens to me, and I know you're my best friend, but even if I told you, you couldn't help what happened. When you were robbed a few years ago and told me, it helped you; but that's not who I am. You know me; I keep things to myself, always have."

"I know you've always been like that. If there's anything I can do please don't hesitate to give me a call."

"Ok Jack. Thanks. I have to get out of here so I can clear my mind. This is the first time in my life I feel like I need a beer."

"Ok pal, I'll talk to you soon, hang in there."

I start walking away from Jack. I need to get out of this place that has completely turned my stomach inside out.

I didn't receive the email and neither did Jack. Both of us are on the board. This seems premeditated. How long did they plan to have this meeting? How far in advance did Sam and Damien have to construct such a slandering ordeal?

I go over to Junior, Rodney's assistant coach who is closer to my age. "I think I need a drink. Do you mind coming with me?" His father Manny, who is also Rodney's assistant, insists to Junior that he goes with me to go grab a few beers at the local bar. I've had enough of this league.

"Yeah let me grab my stuff and we can get out of here."

We start walking to the closest bar from the field, Joe Sent Me. It's only a ten minute walk.

I'm still in shock of what I just found out. I am absolutely irate at this league.

I start to vent to Junior.

"They have no right to talk about me that way. If they had just told me about the meeting and included me in it, I would be able to defend myself. Why hold a secret board meeting about me behind my back?! That's against the law from what I understand. Did Sam do it because he knows I don't have any money to afford a lawyer to sue this league? What was the reason behind it? I'm kind of stuck in no man's land. There were two coaches who told me that they defended me; Adam and Rodney. They were the ones that I know stood up for me."

Junior is getting it from all angles. He knows it's not directed towards him, but I'm telling him how I feel. I'm venting for a change. Rodney and Adam remind me of the incident that occurred when I was an elementary student at the Hale school. Kids were picking on me; Jeff and Anthony came out of nowhere and stopped the bullies from picking on me. I will always remember those who stick up for me. I will never forget Jeff and Anthony for being there for me.

I don't know who else was at the meeting and if there was anything else that was said. The Board of Directors had a secret meeting to discuss the "uprising" of which I've caused. I can't help but think to myself, uprising that *I've* caused? I simply went to a baseball game to talk with the people I know. The last I remember, it's a free country to walk the streets, stop at places of which you enjoy and converse with the people you know.

Are they forgetting that I was the one that had the knife up against my throat? I was the one who was petrified by such a traumatic event. But I guess that had no bearing at the meeting that took place last night. A meeting where they kept calling me a pedophile left and right. I have no idea how many people were sent an email about the meeting, I just know that Jack and I were excluded from the email. It was probably because they knew he and I were such close friends. That could mean close to twenty other members were sent this email and could've been at that meeting.

We arrive at the bar and two seats are available. Before the bartender can ask us anything, I speak first.

"Two bud lights please."

Junior adds, "Frank, I can't drink beer right now. I have to take a test and I can't have any alcohol in my system."

"Not a problem, I'll drink both of them."

I continue my rant about the league.

"I was slandered by my own league for something I've never ever been accused of doing, but yet, the people who I thought of as my family, bashed me in front of the other members that attended this meeting. This meeting only had one topic, me."

292

"During this meeting, it was said that I could be a pedophile. I was held up with a knife back in late May demanding I give the armed and dangerous man money because he thought I got away with being a child molester two years ago. He took the flyer from my car, without my knowledge and premeditated the crime weeks before, forced me into my vehicle, with the knife to my throat and went to the ATMS to take out money. If I didn't cooperate, he said that he would go to the police and tell them that I molested his nephew and swore that he would kill me right then and there."

"He threatened my life if I went to the police about what he did to me; I didn't want to die. So what did I do? I ignored it because I knew it would eventually go away. For two months it went away, but because the league had to get involved, it somehow resurfaced."

"They are going to give me an ultimatum: go to the police and file a report of that incident or the Board of Directors will tell me that I'm resigning! Once I heard about this meeting and the ultimatum that I would be given, I was livid. No one is going to tell me that I can't do anything."

A few minutes go by after I finish my beers.

"Before I have a meeting with Sam and Damien, will you go with me to the police station tomorrow so I can file a report regarding what Terrance did to me?" I ask Junior.

"Yes, I'll go with you just let me know what time."

"Ok, thanks."

Sam and Damien clearly didn't think this through. Either way it doesn't look good on my behalf. If I resign, it looks like

I'm guilty of something. If I file a report, people would start to think I really want to be around kids. This league has now created another misperception, all because Sam was feeling high and mighty with his power.

That son of a bitch has no idea what people will think now. I'm literally in a bind that they caused. Sam let all the power get to his head.

At three o'clock the next day, Junior and I head over to the East Boston police department.

"I'd like to file a report on Terrance Mullins."

"What did he do to you?" The secretary asks.

"He held me up with a knife and demanded money from me. He also sent me a threatening text message. I also have a witness of him bragging about it."

I show her the text messages.

I know ur there, and if you don't call me now then imma fuck ur shit up.

U know how I was saying he officially lost his mind...well apparently Terrance bragged today about robbing you for $2,000.00...he's like a serial killer that wants to get caught. He was saying to tell you to drop the charges or you're gonna be in a world of trouble.

She wrote down both messages and handed my phone back. She wrote down Terrance's number to match it up. She also put Aaron's phone number on the police report.

"Can I have a copy of the report please?"

"Yes you can. A detective will call you in a couple of days."

She hands me a copy of the police report.

I am ready to shove it in Sam and Damien's faces right before they say a word. At that same point, I would like them to push the knife that's already in my back. That way, I can tell them I know what it's like to feel the full wrath of being stabbed completely in the back by a so-called "friend".

I arrive at the park thirty minutes prior to the meeting to watch some of the game so I can relax before I go off on the two of them. Some of my fellow coaches call me a pacifist. But not tonight, this night I need to defend my actions; defend the traumatic events that took place, the pain and suffering I endured not just from being held up, but also what this league has put me through. The time is now for them to see a person they've never seen before. Eight years of being a great coach will show a different side of me tonight that no one else has ever seen.

Both Sam and Damien arrive simultaneously, Damien arriving from the parking lot where I am currently watching the game, and Sam coming from the football field.

Sam starts the conversation.

"Let's take a walk."

I know that he wants us to walk on the other side of the field away from everyone else, in private. It would be just the three of us. I know Sam is doing this on purpose because he doesn't want the people who did attend the meeting to eavesdrop or disrupt us. He doesn't want anyone there to defend me on the spot.

As we are walking together, as quietly as I can, I'm going over in my head what I am about to say. We walk all the way to the other side of the field. People can see us, but there's no one within hearing distance.

"Frank…"

I abruptly interrupt Sam and hand him the police report.

"What is this?"

"This, my friend, is the police report that I filed against the man who committed the crime against me; and you're damn lucky I don't have serving papers to go along with that so I can sue your ass as well!"

Damien looks over to Sam; I can see their cheeks peak the brightest red I've ever seen.

Sam defensively says, "No one was supposed to say anything about the meeting!"

"LEGALLY YOU'RE NOT SUPPOSED TO HAVE A MEETING BEHIND SOMEONE'S BACK AND SLANDER THEM! IF I WERE AT THAT MEETING TO BEGIN WITH, WE WOULDN'T BE HAVING THIS CONVERSATION!"

They look at each other frantically, knowing the fact that they've been caught red handed.

"Sam, as you know, because you are a lawyer, I have quite some time to gather the right witnesses and the right material to sue you and this league if I choose to do so. I just want

296

to make sure that you are aware of what I am capable of, I am telling it as it is right now. I know I have three years to sue your ass for slander. Everyday I'm going to make your life a living hell. I could hand the papers to you right now. But I'd rather have you wait day in and day out asking yourself, is this going to be the day? I know how much of a grace period there is to file a defamation lawsuit. I want to make sure you are aware of this so one day you're not surprised when it comes."

Before Sam can utter any word I interrupt his sentence.

"Now you listen to me for a change. Sam, if you just called me back that Sunday morning I called you, like you said you would, when I received that threatening message from Terrance, maybe I would have some better guidance on how to approach this situation. But no, after I woke you up on a Sunday morning you denied me, despite the fact that you gave me your number to call you anytime. You never called me back like you said you were going to, you asshole."

"WHY WOULD YOU CALL ME ON A SUNDAY MORNING AND NOT THE POLICE?"

"FUCK YOU SAM! YOU TOLD ME TO CALL YOU!"

I continue, "Don't get all defensive on me. Where were you when the flyers were posted up all over the city two years ago?! You said you would handle the matter then, but you didn't. You never had the balls to call me and set up a meeting to talk to you about who I think put up the flyers. I remember when the flyers were posted up on the streets and you said we should sit down somewhere and discuss what happened; you never called me back on that. When I was held up, Damien stated to me that he made you aware of the situation and that if things were to get worse, that I should call you. It got worse and I called you, but you did nothing, you bastard! You are useless to me. Just because I don't make dollar signs appear in your eyes as any stereotypical Jewish person likes to see, you're not willing to help."

Damien starts to get emotional.

"Frank, please calm down."

"CALM DOWN! YOU WANT ME TO CALM DOWN. FUNNY HOW I'M THE ONE THAT GETS THE KNIFE PULLED ON MY NECK. I'M THE ONE THAT'S BEEN FACED WITH AN ABSOLUETLY FICTITIOUS CRIME. I'M THE ONE WITH THE LEAGUE GOING BEHIND MY BACK AND THE COACHES TELLING ME THAT WHAT WAS DISCUSSED THE OTHER NIGHT WAS "NASTY", AND YOU'RE TELLING ME TO CALM DOWN. FUCK YOU BOTH!"

Awkward silence presents itself after I finish defending myself and my actions.

I look over to Damien and say, "Does Damien need a tissue? I'm sorry that Nathan isn't here to pull on your strings. Sam isn't going to comfort you; he's a stone-hearted prick as you already know. As your Puppet Master would say, 'it is what it is.'"

I turn to Sam and say, "You want to have this meeting away from everybody else because you know what you did was wrong. Everyone at that meeting knew what you were doing was a crime in itself. Remember, I can always subpoena them to my liking and if I'm correct, which I know I am, that's all I need to
298

take you both down, take everything you've got. You'll know at that point how it feels to be stripped of your pride. I've said what I needed to say. You've got your police report. Just remember, I now have the upper hand, so before you make another bad decision, think about the consequences. It's funny, I never did anything wrong, but this league has many coaches who smoke marijuana before they coach a game, you have an alcoholic coach who is drunk during most of his practices and games. You have someone who sells marijuana, and you even had a coach who would hit a player on their ass after every single play, and they're still coaching. With me, I did nothing wrong. I don't smoke, I very rarely drink. I don't do drugs and MORE IMPORTANTLY I'M NOT A PEDOPHILE, YOU ASSHOLES!"

I walk away bullshit with Sam and Damien. I've never been this frustrated before in my life.

The closest to an argument that I've been in was when I was eighteen and my mother yelled at me, which is very rare for her to do to me. I didn't yell back, I just walked out of the house and didn't say a word. I knew she was wrong. Within a couple of hours she realized she was wrong. She called me and apologized for her behavior. It's not often I get upset, but when I do, I'm proving a point.

I leave without saying a word to anyone else. I just go right to my car and drive away.

I am exhausted in so many ways. I want to quit coaching, but I know that's what they want me to do. They are not going to get that satisfaction. I don't deserve this from anyone; especially those who I thought were close to me. The same league that has helped me stop being shy; is now tearing me down, piece by piece, day by day.

Still recovering from the psychological damage, it feels like someone blindsided me, kicked me while I was down, the blood dripping down slowly from my many wounds, I feel completely stripped of my pride. These mental beatings feel physical. Burning the wounds with salt; who I once believed to be a family to me, has completely turned on me. No justice, no self-righteous explanation, just a pure beating on an innocent man.

CHAPTER FORTY-FIVE

The next day, Rodney forwards me an email from Damien.

To the Board of Directors:

Frank, Sam, and I discussed the matter regarding the situation that has occurred over the past few weeks.

After having the meeting with Frank; Sam and I believe that Frank's maturity has grown by the conclusion of the meeting. As we discussed at our Board meeting days ago, Sam and I have agreed to keep Frank as the manager of the Giants. We feel going forward that Frank will make better decisions and that the previous incident will be behind us.

If there is anyone who wasn't at the meeting and would like us to discuss these events that have occurred

*please feel free to give me a call or send me an email and
I will gladly get you up to speed on the matter at hand.*

*Also, if anyone believes Frank shouldn't be
coaching in Cambridge anymore, send me an email or
call me and I can reassure you that Frank is fit to stay as
the manager of the Giants.*

*Thanks for being patient for this difficult yet
important situation that has arisen.*

Yours Truly,
Damien

Once I read this message, my first thought is, "My
maturity has grown?"

How mature were they to go behind my back and defame
me? Clearly that's evident enough that I am much more mature
than Sam and Damien on how I handled the matter.

I can't believe they said that. I can't believe they are
willing to talk to anyone who wants to hear about something that
isn't even true. I can't believe they were so gullible to listen to
whatever Lisa's fiancé; Ben's coach, had to say because they
were falling for that bitch's antics.

They are sugar coating what was discussed in the meeting
to make themselves look better. That email was sent to twenty
members. There is no doubt in my mind that everyone will
believe the email. This is just what I need, more people knowing
what they don't need to know; it is my life, not theirs. But
curiosity will get the best of them, as it always does.

If I were at that meeting, I'm sure I could've made sense of the topic at hand. But they never gave me a chance to explain or even identify the craziness of Lisa's behavior. Those who saw her at my field during the All-Star game two years ago saw how crazy she can be.

Sam or Damien never attended that game but they got to take charge of an ungodly meeting without knowing the other party's behavior. Another classless move made by two classless people.

Not only does Sam and Damien think they knew what happened to me, but other members of the board now know that I was held up and that my freedom to go anywhere is being taken away. I haven't done anything wrong, but everyone is assuming I've done something wrong. This meeting will only create a bad chain of events. People keeping secrets, that never happens. Someone will talk sometime and when they do, people will assume they know what happened and listen to the rumors and not the facts.

Since the league decided to share information with everyone, without the necessary precautions, they might as well have held a press conference at city hall. They can call it "The Defamation" and it will be a special on ESPN so that everyone can see how badly the league bent me over a thousand times. Oh wait, they might think I would enjoy that. I don't know what the difference would be. The league already had a meeting that consisted of lies. It was only a matter of time before someone started believing those lies. There is always someone somewhere who will believe in false information.

No one sees the pain and suffering that I have endured through this time of my life. Because of what happened with Terrance, I dealt with a hostile environment for two months amongst people that should not have been part of my experience as a victim. Everything was fine until the league got involved. I knew what I was doing. Someone else should not get involved with another's life when they have no idea of what is going on, they should just leave it be.

I see Mr. Loney the next day on my way to the afterschool program.

"Were you at the meeting the other night?"

"Yes I was."

"Can you tell me who was there?"

"No, I can't. But if you came to us in the beginning, we would've been able to help you."

"I came to the league right away and this is what you guys did to me. The league went behind my back and defamed my character. Everyone should be ashamed of how they conducted themselves."

"You went to Sam and Damien when it happened?"

"Yes Mr. Loney. The day it happened I called Damien within hours of the incident. Now I regret doing so but it's too late."

He's completely stone faced. He's unaware that I did go to the league right away for advice. He's suddenly embarrassed that he opened his big mouth without knowing the truth.

"I'm sorry." He slowly turns around disappointed.

He starts walking away with his head down. Now he's aware that what he and the other members at the meeting did, what the league did, was wrong.

It made me understand that I had to do everything on my own. No one cared about what happened to me, they just cared about what they thought was better for the league. But they never knew about the other coaches, the ones who smoked marijuana before games, the alcoholic coach, and more importantly, they never said anything to Jerry who always hit the players on the ass after every play. If anyone had any inclination of being a pedophile, it would be him.

No one can predict the future, they can only assume what they think might happen. Next time anyone has anything to say, they better make sure they know all the facts instead of making assumptions. It seems that's what this league thrives on.

My life is shattered into a million pieces, with no fault of my own. Truthfully, Sam and Damien are assholes. Anyone with power and authority feels like they can get away with anything until their mistakes are known publicly.

The detective that's on the case regarding Terrance calls me. "Is this Frank Grover?"

"Yes, this is."

"Frank, this is Detective Leone. I was wondering if you could get a copy of your phone records, your bank statements, and with your permission, a look at your phone."

"I have nothing to hide detective. How far back do you want?"

"I just need the past three months."

"Not a problem. Even though I know I'm innocent, I want you to be honest with me."

"What do you mean?"

"Did you talk to the Cambridge police about the flyer?"

"Yes I did. They were not happy about this incident that happened to you."

"They weren't happy with me? If they just did their job to serve and protect the innocent maybe we wouldn't be in this situation. I'm sure they want to see my records to make sure the flyers don't indicate what is being said. Like I said before, I've got nothing to hide. You can have the phone records, the bank records, and you can even check my phone. Like I told Terrance, I didn't do anything, but yet I'm the one that is the victim. I'll drop them off to you as soon as I can. Do you need anything else from me?"

"No, that will be it."

It pissed me off that they wanted to check everything, but at the same time I knew it would only vindicate me. I hadn't done anything wrong, but everyone still had this perception. Even the Cambridge police department was upset that Terrance held me up. If they did their job the right way, Ashley would've been arrested and I wouldn't be in this position. But they insisted there wasn't any surveillance. Over ten locations had cameras and I found it very strange that none of them worked. The fingerprints were on the flyer but they couldn't get the culprit. None of this added up. Was the Cambridge Police department upset that someone else knew about it because of their mishap?

I sent in all the paper work that the detective wanted and I even highlighted when Terrance called me the day he held me up. I highlighted the locations of the bank when the money was taken out. It identifies the time and place which coincided with what I told the detective. He should be able to get video surveillance of that as well.

Now I have to try and focus on the All-Star game. My team, the Giants, won the division and as a result, we as a staff get to coach the All-Star team. The All-Star game is in September and I must not show the distaste I have for the league at this time. I can't quit. Not yet. I still have a team I need to represent in the All-Star game. It's the best season I've had as a manager, but the worst personally.

CHAPTER FORTY-SIX

Mancini's denied my unemployment benefits. I have a hearing in a couple of days and I've gathered everything I can in order to fight their decision. I gathered my telephone records, my bank statements, everything I can to support the fact that I was only doing what I was told to do. I have the option of electing someone to represent me. For what I've been through in the past two years, I can't rely on anyone. I have to do this alone. It's the only way I believe it will be done right.

It's a four o'clock appointment on a Wednesday afternoon. I arrive at 3:30. I'm always early. Everyone is dressed in business attire. I walk into the room wearing a graphic t-shirt and jeans.

I walk over to the secretary.

"Hi, I'm Frank Grover and I have an appointment at four."

"Yes Frank, would you like to see your file?"

"Yes please, I would appreciate it."

I read that Mancini's says I didn't follow the correct procedures.

"Can I have copies of these?"

"Yes you may."

"Thanks."

The secretary makes copies and then hands them to me after she is done. As she is handing me the copies I see Miranda walking into the room.

"How you are doing Frank?"

"I'm hanging in there."

"I heard what Terrance did to you."

"Yet Aaron tells me that he's still working at the store. That makes perfect sense."

"Still a smart ass I see."

"The best you'll ever encounter."

"We have to see how it pans out with Terrance before we can do anything."

"Funny, I thought I was following protocol according to what Colin said. You think I'm wrong and you fire me. But when someone gets arrested for committing a crime, they continue to work at your store. Yes, it definitely makes perfect sense to me."

Burt walks into the room. The unbiased representative from unemployment services arrives. He asks to see Miranda and Burt first. They talk for ten minutes and then the representative comes out and says I can come in now.

The hearing lasts longer than anticipated, an hour passes and it's the end of the day for the representative. Miranda, Burt, and I have agreed to continue this in a couple of weeks, on a Friday morning.

For weeks, I am barely making it financially. I have the after-school program but I'm only making $200.00 per paycheck. My rent is $400.00 a month. Half of what I make goes to rent each month. I barely eat because I can't afford it. Larry and his wife notice my lack of nutrition.

"Frank, we've noticed that you haven't looked well."

Larry's wife cares; she knows how hard it is to make a living. With the situation I am trying to fight with Mancini's for the past twelve weeks, I can barely afford to pay rent but I manage to survive.

"To be honest, I don't eat much. I don't have the money right now to do it."

She turns to Larry, "Let's go to Star Market and help him out a bit."

"Frank, you should file for government assistance. If it wasn't for that, we don't know how we would survive. You would qualify for something but I'm not sure how much."

"Where is it? I really don't know how much longer I can go on like this."

"It's in Revere. Larry will take you tomorrow if you'd like."

"I appreciate it guys. I really do."

"No problem Frank. You were there for us. It's time we return the favor."

We go to Star Market and I still feel bad that they are using their funds for me, so I keep it at a bare minimum: bread, peanut butter, a few cold cuts and Coca-Cola. I didn't want to buy the coke, but they insisted on it. They knew how much I enjoy Coca-Cola. It ended up being $45.00 worth of food. It wasn't a lot to them but it was to me. I never ask for anything from anyone and I felt embarrassed that someone was helping me out.

"Are you sure this is all you want Frank?"

"This is all I need. It's more than enough."

Within a couple of days, the government approved a $200.00 food stamp balance per month. I was relieved. It helped me tremendously. I didn't like the fact that I was on food stamps but at this point, it would help me survive and I couldn't thank Larry and his wife enough for helping me out through this process. I have my meeting with Mancini's and the unemployment office tomorrow morning.

I arrive at the unemployment office at 10:30 am, a half hour early. Burt and Miranda walk in, but this time they brought Colin with them.

Miranda, Burt, and I are arguing about the events that took place. When it was time for me to ask questions, I directed them towards Colin.

"Colin, when I called you that day about the money order, you told me I could either replace the money order with the cash, if I have it on me, or I can cash it at the bank and put it in the daily deposit."

"I never told you to put it in your name."

"How else would I cash it?"

"You put Mancini's name on the money order."

"You never said that."

311

"I don't remember that conversation to be honest with you Frank."

"Do you remember when I asked you about stamps and how to go about that process? I didn't know how to put it in the system to take the cash out and buy the stamps but you told me how to do it."

"Yes, I remember that conversation."

"The question prior to that had to do with the money order."

"I don't remember."

I take out the phone records and I highlight his phone number. I show everyone the twenty minute conversation we had.

"That conversation wasn't just about stamps."

The representative listens to both sides and at the conclusion of the meeting he states, "I will look over the evidence that is presented before me."

He turns to me, "If your claim is denied you have a right to appeal. Likewise Miranda and Burt, you can appeal the decision as well."

I walk out of the room, still acting like the nicest guy to all three of them. I'm still a nice guy and I always will be. We're talking as if we are friends, as if the hearing never took place.

CHAPTER FORTY-SEVEN

Late August we start practicing for the All-Star game which occurs the weekend after Labor Day. Aaron, Jim's mother, Cedric, and Andre's father are helping me set up the practices. Nobody knows what happened last month. None of the parents or coaches that are a part of this team is aware of the way the league has slandered my reputation. It is the first time I'm on the field since I had the meeting with Sam and Damien.

I really don't want to be here. I just want to get this over and done with. But I can't stop thinking of what they did to me and all the people who ask me questions and give me weird looks. It's only one or two games at best. It's the last tournament I will ever coach in this city. I can hang in there for just a few more weeks.

The first week in September I receive a letter from the Division of Unemployment:

It has been determined that after the testimonial from both sides, and the evidence that was brought to my attention, I have decided to approve the unemployment claim favoring the claimant. The evidence that favored the claimant was the testimonial from the training supervisor.

After recalling the conversation that Frank and the training supervisor had, the training supervisor did not recall the conversation regarding the money order but he did with the stamp. The training manager specifically said: "I don't remember." It suggested that Frank was right in the miscommunication that took place when a duplicate money order was printed by accident. The phone records also indicated a lengthy conversation.

For that reason, it was enough to suggest Frank was wrongfully fired for a miscommunication and negligence from the company. All funds will be awarded in retro for each week that was claimed from the week Frank was let go.

I won the appeal. I knew I was right and I proved it. By myself, the only way I knew I could win this battle. The funds would be deposited in my bank account within a week. That's $5,000.00.

Because I won the appeal, Kim told me that I can only work one day a week at the school. The City of Cambridge doesn't want to pay me twice; once from unemployment and the other when I am working with the school. I am now just working on Friday afternoons.

I have the All-Star game this weekend; this will most likely be my last tournament as a coach for this league. I've held on long enough. I don't think I can handle any more at this point. I'm completely drained by all the things I have had to deal with.

I don't remember the All-Star game. I remember being on the field and eventually losing 4 – 2 but that's it. I tried to coach the game, but I was at a loss for words. I didn't have any motivation. Knowingly convincing myself that this was probably my last game, I just didn't know how to retire. I don't quit anything. I don't know how to do it. Deep down, I still want to be here. I still want to coach. But with all I have been through over the past two years, I just don't think I can go through anything else without snapping.

CHAPTER FORTY-EIGHT

Since I believe this is going to be my last year, I buy each coach a handmade jacket with the Giants logo, their name on the sleeve and Cambridge Division Champs 2011, to thank them for the season that we had as a team. I want to give them something that will remind them of the success we had.

Receiving the league trophy at the banquet is the highlight of the worst year I had personally. The entire coaching staff bought the players t-shirts to remind them of the successful season we had. There was still a part of me that wanted to stay and coach. But the flyers that Ashley posted had created the chain of events that he intended on.

One week passes since the banquet, Larry and his wife invite me over for lunch on a Saturday afternoon. I arrive at the house and Larry says to me, "I have to go pick up my kids' friends, do you want to come along or do you want to stay here with my wife? I shouldn't be too long."

Before I can say anything, Justin flies down the stairs.

"Do you want to play Madden on the Xbox 360?"

"Frank that's fine, go play Madden with Justin and I'll be back soon."

As we are playing Madden, the game freezes up. I take the disk out and I try to rub out the scratches that are on it. As I put the disk back in, Justin jumps on my back.

The momentum of his weight makes me fall backwards. I land on my back, on the bed. I break out of his headlock and I put him in a headlock. As I am trying to lift him up to body slam him, I notice that he's holding on the mattress with both hands. I try lifting him and as I am doing so, Larry's wife comes walking in the room.

"What are you doing?"

"We're wrestling. The game froze and he jumped on my back so I tried picking him up to body slam him onto the bed."

"That isn't what you were doing."

"What are you implying?"

"It didn't look like wrestling to me." She grabs her son and heads downstairs. "You don't wrestle with a fourteen year-old!"

"He jumped on my back! I don't see what the big deal is."

"We are going to wait for Larry to come home."

"Are you accusing me of doing something, because if you are, come out and say it."

"It just didn't look right."

"You know what? We can wait for Larry, that's fine by me. I know I didn't do anything wrong. That baseball a couple of months ago clearly did some damage to your brain."

"You should know better!"

"You're right I should have known how much of a bitch you are, considering that's what everyone has been telling me. Even your own parents said you're a bitch and they love Larry more than you. I should've listened to the people who were telling me that you were trouble. I was told you have a history. Maybe I was naïve to think it wouldn't happen to me because I know I'm a nice guy, but I guess with you, history repeats itself."

"Get the fuck out of my house!"

"My pleasure, you bitch."

As I am walking out, Larry arrives at the house.

"I feel bad for you. You have a complete bitch for a wife. I can't take it anymore. Justin jumped on my back after the Madden game froze, and your wife is accusing me of doing something I didn't do."

"Do you want to talk about it?"

"She's just a bitch Larry, there's nothing I can do about that. I should've listened to the coaches about her but I didn't. I didn't think it would happen. But I'm going home to figure out what they are talking about. Your marriage is more important than my friendship. I do appreciate all that you've done for me."

I left in a complete daze that Larry's wife just accused me of such actions. Nothing even seemed remotely close to her accusations.

As I arrive to my house, I decide to look up her name.

A few years ago she accused a hockey coach of abusing her son. It was all over the news. She filed a report on him. It was later dropped because there wasn't any evidence. It was all over the news and I never knew about it. To be honest, I never watch the news. I was coaching in the league at that time. That coach continued to coach hockey, but Larry and his wife went to a different hockey league for their son and daughters.

I can't believe she had the audacity to blame me for something I didn't do. But I guess that comes with the territory of being a bitch. Even her parents couldn't stand her. They said she was a bitch and that Larry deserves better. There were plenty of times I could tell Larry didn't want to be in the relationship. But he didn't have anywhere else to go. He loves his children; he didn't want to split up with his wife because he didn't know how often he would see his children if they got divorced. He continually dealt with her attitude, because he didn't have much of a choice. Larry's wife believed in the rumors that the league created. The flyers that were posted a couple of years ago created that illusion.

The rumors have spread like wildfire since the league created that secret meeting about me. When Sam and Damien told the other members of the board that night to not speak of this meeting to anyone, it became clear that the league enabled this misperception of me. This is the second time I am accused of being a pedophile, this time it is as bad as it will ever get.

Kim calls me the day before I am supposed to be at work.

"Frank, I received a call from the office. My boss told me that you're on leave until an investigation is done."

319

"Really, are you kidding me?"

"Yes, that's what they told me. I told them you only work here one day anyway."

"That son of a bitch, I can't believe Larry's wife would do that."

"I'm sorry Frank."

I hung up the phone. I couldn't believe Larry's wife would go that far. She was wrong.

Shouldn't all the coaches who have a tendency to smack their player's butts for a good job be investigated and interviewed as well? I have never hit anyone on their butt nor would I ever, but a coach who consistently did it in Cambridge was never asked to stop nor was he ever investigated. Where's the justice in that?! No one should hit any child on the butt after a play!

What about all the coaches who teach kids wrestling, should they be investigated as well? I was defamed. I was robbed with assault and battery with a knife, but because I was the victim in all this, the league made me out to be something that I'm really not.

CHAPTER FORTY-NINE

I was so fed up with the league that I decided to go visit my Aunt and Uncle. Since all my immediate family members lived in Texas, this was the closest relative for me to go to. Because of the school doing an investigation, I thought it would be helpful to vent to someone outside of the league. Spending time with people who love and appreciate me temporarily numbs the pain.

As I am talking to my Aunt, I begin to tell her of the false accusations made by somebody who had a history of falsely accusing coaches in the past. This is a person who was supposedly my "friend"; a person who had just recently helped me out during my financial crisis.

My aunt knows that I am not capable of such a crime. After listening to what I have to say, she smiles and says, "Let's go out. We need to go out somewhere, to get your mind off of things."

She tells her husband that she is going out with me, her daughter, and granddaughter. We end up going to Oyes Restaurant, a sushi bar.

As we are talking at the table, I ask the waitress if they can change the channel to watch the season premiere of *Grimm*. To no avail, they do not change it. After having a few drinks, the waiter brings over a platter with 100% proof alcohol in the middle of it, where they light it on fire. After sharing an absolutely hilarious evening of laughing and joking with my aunt and two cousins, I decide to drink the alcohol before they come light it on fire.

The waiter frantically yells, "No, no, no! Don't do that!"

By that time, it was too late, I already drank it.

We are enjoying one another's company and having a great time throughout the night. Despite my crazy antics and obvious drunkenness, my aunt praises all of us and confesses that this is the most fun she's had in a very long time. This is something I need, considering what I had just been through. It is great to have a fun night out with people who care about me. I ask my aunt if it is alright for me to sleep over. I have never slept over her house before, but I'm so drunk that I'm not going to drive under any circumstances.

"Of course! You're always welcome to stay over! I wouldn't want you to drive anyway." My aunt is more than happy to assist me.

We arrive back at the house around 10:15 pm. I am already beginning to feel the effects of the hangover, but I don't care because I had such a good time as did everybody else. I decide that the only way to recover from a night like this is to go to bed early. I say goodnight to everybody and thank them for such a good time. My aunt insists that there is no need to say thank you because she had the time of her life.

It's 12:15 in the morning and I am awakened by a loud *BANG* followed by my aunt screaming my name. I go running to assist her, to see what all of the ruckus is about. She's in her husband's bedroom trying to lift him from his apparent kneeling position. His head is on the night stand and his body is slouched over; he has fallen. Blood is coming from his forehead.

There is no response.

My aunt, frantic, says "Call 911. He's not breathing."

Within minutes, the EMT arrives and he's being rushed to the hospital. My aunt and her daughter go to the hospital, and I stay behind to make sure that my cousin is ok.

We later find out that my uncle has had a heart attack and died. He was dead before we called 911. It's difficult to process, considering just hours before we were out having the greatest time of our lives with one another. I can't help but think it has something to do with me.

It seems that no matter what I do or where I go, misery follows me. This is the first time I've ever slept over and the night ends in tragedy. Nothing ever seems to go right for me these days.

CHAPTER FIFTY

The next day Jerry Sandusky is all over the news. The biggest scandal in Penn State history is on every news channel and every sports channel.

I've had enough of this. I can't bear to be part of the City of Cambridge anymore. I am so sick and tired of the perception that has been created ever since those flyers were posted. I can only imagine the jokes that may follow with the Jerry Sandusky incident. I can just picture Adam or anyone saying something like: "Jerry Sandusky isn't your father is he?" I don't want to see anyone from Cambridge anymore.

On November 5th, I finally decide that I can't deal with what Ashley did to me and the chain of events that followed: The jokes, Terrance, Sam and Damien's meeting and now Larry's wife. I have no other choice. I can't deal with this anymore. I have to walk away from this.

I send the following email to Damien and Kim:

I'm emotionally, physically, and mentally drained. I can't do this anymore. I'm done.

That is all I write. That's how I feel. After sending this email to Kim and Damien, it feels bitter-sweet. My life as a coach is over. Albeit in the coaching world, the past three years were my most successful out of the eight years that I was a coach, emotionally and mentally it was one of the worst periods of my life. After a record of 38 – 41 in the regular season and a 10 – 4 record in the playoffs (7 – 1 the past three years); two playoff championships and a Division champ trophy, this is it. This is when I say goodbye. For all those who care, I am finally leaving the league. I would have loved to eventually coach in college or maybe even the pros one day, but I just can't deal with it anymore at this point in time.

The few people I saw after Larry's wife accused me said they knew she was wrong. She talked about it for a little while, but once her son was interviewed, she knew she was wrong, again. They were telling me that Larry was upset with his wife that she would even pursue anything against me. He knew I wouldn't do anything to his son. He's been through this ordeal before and he was sick and tired of the way she acted. However, he loved his family so he chose to deal with the horrible days with his wife; it was better than having nobody.

I receive a text message from Larry's wife two weeks after she accuses me:

"I think it is best that we no longer be friends."

I don't respond to it. This right here tells me she is wrong. I delete it right then and there. She knows she is wrong and she doesn't even apologize. She is too stubborn and won't admit it when she is wrong. It doesn't matter anymore. The damage is done.

It takes the league three weeks to respond to the email and Damien doesn't even send it himself, he has Sam send the email:

Frank:

Damien forwarded your email of November 5, 2011 to me and we had a long talk about it. I am sorry you are feeling completely drained. I appreciate and admire that you have decided to withdraw from the league to concentrate on your own life and needs. Damien and I think it is best that you devote your strength and energy to restoring yourself at this time. On behalf of the league and Damien, as President, we accept your resignation from the Board and as coach of the Giants. Accordingly, I ask you to not come to the Board meeting on Thursday, Dec. 1.

We thank you for your efforts on behalf of the league and your team and hope that your resignation will provide you the time to help restore your mental, emotional and physical strength.

Sincerely,
Sam

Again, Damien couldn't send the letter himself, he was ashamed for slandering my name and my reputation because of the ungodly meeting that should've never taken place.

I'd finally given up; all that I'd enjoyed throughout the eight years that I'd coached in the league was over. It was simply time to move on. Some people thought that I quit, on the contrary; there's a difference between giving up and knowing when you've had enough. After two long years of battling the defamation, the two long years of suffering from people who at one time I considered a family, going behind my back and creating ungodly rumors, I had enough.

The professionalism of the league was more like high school teenagers being bullies, creating teenage nonsense rumors. I had enough of that when I was in high school, but I couldn't walk away then; this time I could walk away.

Cambridge should be ashamed of how they handled such a horrific ordeal on one of their own. It's no surprise to me why three of the Board of Directors quit shortly after the closed-door meeting of that I was not asked to attend. It's no surprise why one of the Board of Directors and his wife took their kids out of the program and also quit coaching. They knew what happened to me wasn't right.

I was depressed, I had lost everything. It was the first time in a very long time that I had absolutely nothing to do. No job, no school, and no team to coach. Every day I would just stay in bed. I lost twenty pounds. My doctor was worried that I could be clinically depressed. He prescribed me drugs; Adderall and Lorazepam. But I refused to take any medication.

On a whim, I decide to drive to Texas and surprise my family for Christmas.

My mother had moved down to Texas a year ago; where she was a full time grandmother and my brother moved there six years ago with his wife. I left on Dec 17th, a Saturday afternoon at four. Traffic wouldn't be too bad at that hour.

I had a thirty hour drive ahead of me. I had nothing else going on for me at home. It was something I could use. My family didn't know I was on my way. I packed a cooler with drinks and some snacks for the long trip ahead of me.

Six hours into my drive, in Pennsylvania, I see a police car with its lights flashing behind me. I realize he's pulling me over.

"License and registration."

"Did I do something wrong?"

"Do you know how fast you were going?"

"Obviously not fast enough considering there was a car right in front of me."

"Don't get smart with me."

"I'm not being smart. I'm telling you I wasn't going as fast as you think because someone was right in front of me. I honestly think you pulled over the wrong person."

The officer heads over to his patrol car.

I knew I wasn't going that fast. Maybe ten miles over the speed limit but that's about it. I'm not in a rush to get to Texas. I am enjoying my time on the road.

The police officer comes back to my car.

"Where are you going?"

328

"I am on my way to Texas to visit my family."

"You are coming from Massachusetts?"

"That's what my license says, right?"

"Don't be a fucking smartass punk!"

"You may think I'm being a smartass but if you really think about it, I am only stating the obvious. You are the one asking stupid questions."

He gave me a ticket for $185.00 dollars. I didn't care if I was telling the truth, I didn't deserve the ticket. I knew he has the wrong person, so I was going to appeal the ticket.

Six more hours on the road and I call it quits for the night. I'm staying in the great state of Virginia on my first night of my road trip.

The next day as I am driving through Tennessee, I head over the bridge in Nashville and see that it is an absolutely beautiful city at night. I am going to have to make a separate trip down here at some point in my life. I want to make sure I have time to go Christmas shopping once I surprise my family in Texas.

Fifteen more hours on the road and I stop at a hotel in Texarkana, Arkansas. Tomorrow morning I will only have about a four hour drive ahead of me. I'm going to surprise my mother at work.

As I head into Dallas, I know I have to find a Dunkin Donuts before I stop in to surprise my mother. One thing is for sure, she loves her coffee.

I walk into her store and I head towards the back of the store. Someone walks out of the storage room.

"Excuse me, is Jennie here?"

"Yes, she's in the back. Can I help you with something?"

"I was wondering if you can take me to where she is. I'm her son and I drove all the way from Massachusetts to see her. She doesn't know I'm here. I'm Frank."

"She'll be excited to see you! She always talks about you!"

She takes me to my mother.

"Jennie, someone is here to see you."

She turns around and is surprised to see me.

"When did you get here?"

"Just now, here's your coffee. I drove down here."

"I can't believe you're here. How long will you be here?"

"I'll be spending a couple weeks here."

"What about work?"

"I have some time off from work."

I didn't tell her what happened to me, not yet anyway. I'll survive just like I have in the past. Unfortunately, it's something I've grown accustomed to.

I spent a lot of money on my nephew, my brother, my sister-in-law, my aunt, and my mother for Christmas. I don't care about money. I don't have a lot but any chance I get to spend it on everyone else, I cherish it.

The best gift I gave out was to my brother and mother. I put it in a Christmas card and addressed it to both of them. My brother didn't know what it could be, and after looking at it, he handed it to my mother.

"This is addressed to the both of us, I don't know why, but you can open it."

She opens the card, "It is three tickets to see the Boston Bruins play the Dallas Stars on New Year's Eve."

"Bruins tickets!" my brother shows his excitement for the gift.

"I was going to get tickets but we ended up not getting them." My brother explains.

I look over to my sister-in-law, I can tell she wants to go but I didn't know who would take care of the baby.

"I'm sorry I didn't get four tickets but I didn't know who would take care of the baby. As much I really wanted to get four tickets, I didn't know who would babysit."

"It's ok Frank, I understand."

This trip was something I needed. It gave me an insight of the people that do care about me. After all that I'd been through, I'd decided to cut ties with just about everyone who was part of Cambridge. I blocked nearly thirty people on Facebook and I deleted five close friends; even Jack and Aaron.

It was part of my New Year's resolution. After losing my job at Mancini's, I didn't have insurance to go forward with the jaw surgery that I was supposed to have a few months ago. That is something else I need to work on this year.

My drive back to Massachusetts taught me a few things.

For the first time I'm rolling up my sleeves. For all those behind me; let me take charge. I've had enough of holding back. It's time I start to speak up. Time to show everyone that I'm ready to fight back because it's my life they destroyed and it's worth fighting for. There's no happy ending because I can never have my life back to the way it was before.

Distance from the league was the best thing I could do. After dealing with depression, I finally realized I was just surrounded by a bunch of assholes. I'll be coming back better than ever. I'm finally going to break out of my shell. This rat is finally coming out of his cage. It's time to speak up. It's time for everyone to know what I went through and how I survived such traumatic events. I'm curious to see their reactions once the truth comes out. The truth, I have heard, will set me free.

After many months of hitting rock bottom because of Sam and Damien and their meeting they had, Sam's last words to me in the email have stuck in my brain since I have been trying to rejuvenate myself. Looking back at Sam's last email to me, I am able to read between his lines. It's because of him that I felt completely drained.

Let it be known that I will devote my strength and energy to restoring myself in a way that he could never imagine. I will come back better than ever. My resignation will provide me the time to restore my mental, emotional and physical strength. Now I know what I must do. It's time for the truth to come out.

Throughout my life, I have always taken the high road; being a special needs student during my school years, being made fun of constantly in high school; bullies smashing hard covered books over my head, pouring gallons of cologne on me, pushing me into lockers and calling me rat face every day.

For all those times, I never clenched a fist, or even fought back one bit. I took the beating day in and day out.

This incident is just like the ones in the past; picked on by people older than me, bossing me around, spreading rumors and beating up on me mentally. Although it feels like a physical beating, I've wiped off whatever pride there was left and finally walked away. I threw in the white towel.

In the end, it doesn't even matter. People will say I gave up, but the bottom line is, I never gave up, I walked away because I finally had enough.

If a city can sweep their fellow friend's mistake under the rug, they've done it to the wrong victim. I am not going to take any of this lightly anymore. This was once a losing battle for me whichever path I took. If I were to sue the non-profit league for defamation, it would cause the league to collapse and the kids would eventually be out on the streets getting into who knows what. This would make me the bad guy and put me at fault. It would be a lost cause. I had already tried to go to the police once the flyers were posted and even though I knew who was at fault, they still did nothing to help my cause. I tried to talk to Sam, the lawyer of the league since Damien insisted I did. Sam wanted nothing to do with it. No other lawyer wanted to help me out because I couldn't front any money. I have had enough with the police, lawyers, and league officials.

There's no doubt in my mind that if the league didn't care so much about the B team winning in the summer league in 2008, this would have never happened. I would have never dated Lisa. Ashley would've never posted those flyers all around the City of Cambridge. Terrance would've never have seen the flyer and the false accusations it proclaimed and he would have never put the knife to my neck and assaulted me. The league would not have had a secret meeting to defame me even further. Since the secret meeting had witnesses who could report a crime of slander, everyone knew that someone would talk at some point. My friends that were present in the meeting told me what happened because they knew that what was said in the meeting was wrong. Once it leaked out, it created another false perception. After being so irate with the league at that point, I didn't know what to do. Soon after that, the rumors spread about what was talked about in the meeting which later turned into a false accusation.

This ultimately made me want to get out of a league in order for the perceptions to dwindle, because unfortunately with any rumor, someone somewhere will always think it is true. It's sad to realize that everyone forgot who I was. For the past two years everyone has been remembering who I am not.

What Ashley did to me is his best kept secret but I'm going to be his biggest mistake. What he doesn't know is that he tried to destroy my life, but it didn't work. He finally succeeded in having me retire from the league, but that was his only pleasure in it all because I'm going to make every effort to come back.

Ashley needed to be a real man and stop acting like the little bitch that he was; he needed to face the music the right way. Ashley will never admit his mistake. It's quite evident he didn't finish high school. It must have been tough for him to live knowing that he'd be stupid and uneducated for the rest of his life; once he realized that, he became a bully to everyone and anyone around him.

He might've gotten the best of me for a while, but now there is only one thing that I can do that will get him. The truth will be known. Once it is, the eye of the storm will pass over him and all hell will break loose and when it does, he won't have anyone or anything to go to.

If the league stands there and does nothing, they know they were wrong. If they decide to do something about it, the witnesses and evidence I have against them will eventually come full circle. Stuck in a predicament, more of an ultimatum, this is one for them to answer for. Which choice would be more excruciating to deal with? This, my friend, will be the biggest decision that they will ever make. They might as well have another meeting about me, but this time it's for how they want to handle my recourse to their actions. Now I know every person who was at that meeting: Kim, Melissa, Mr. Loney, Rodney, Adam, and three others. Sam and Damien don't know that I know everyone who attended that slandering meeting. There's a fire burning in the middle of the rain; they can't put it out this time.

It's time I give everyone the proverbial middle finger. For too long I've been taking their bullshit but now I'm done with it. If anyone is going to talk about me, I'm going to give them a real reason to do so. People always look out for the quiet man, but it's the man who's been quiet for too long that they should be worried about.

ACKNOWLEDGEMENTS

I could not have done this without my mother. She always gave me that extra push when everything seemed impossible. She passed away suddenly, shortly before the release of this book. She was 57 years young.

Ma, I know you are somewhere looking out after me. Thanks for everything, I love you.

Monica: Thank you for all your hard work on being my first editor. I truly appreciate all that you have done for me. You are the best sister-in-law anyone can ask for! Thanks for everything.

Julie: My second editor, you critiqued my book while having the best possible unbiased opinion. You helped me shed a light on certain things that needed clarification. You gave me that extra push to insert a chapter that you deemed necessary. Thank you for all your hard work.

Michael: Thank you for dedicating your time in proofreading the final edition before the release. Your candid review wraps up the story in a way like no other. I can't thank you enough.

Johnathan and Chris: My brothers, you both helped me with my lacking website skills. Thank you for getting my website up and running.

My Father: Thanks Dad for being there for me when I needed it the most. When you said you liked the book, I was ecstatic. That meant a lot to me, coming from you.

Eddie: You were a voice when I needed it the most. I cannot thank you enough be being there for me.

Bill: Thank you for hearing me out when I needed someone to talk to. You were another voice giving their opinion when times were rough.

Thank you to everyone who had a part of this story in one way or another. My influence didn't just come from my mother; it also came from those of you who were there for me, especially when I didn't think anyone was.

ABOUT THE AUTHOR

Frank Grover is in his early thirties. He has an ardent passion for sports of any kind whether it is coaching, playing or watching. Many say he is a secretive person, but he just has a difficult time opening himself up to others. Underneath his easygoing demeanor, is a heartfelt devoted man who is loyal to a fault and would do anything for the ones he loves.

Frank currently lives in Massachusetts.